FOREWORD

CAPITAL BANK is proud of its people, and of its investment in their personal development.

As an organisation we believe that training is the key, not only to unlocking the potential of each staff member, but also to satisfying the individual requirements of our clients.

The CAPITAL BANK Foundation Building is a unique symbol of our commitment to these principles. Although a Centre of Excellence for training in its own right, the building is also a place where imagination and creativity are encouraged to play a part in the learning process.

The emphasis on the importance of nurturing the human spirit has been created through the work of sculptor Stephen Broadbent. His central 'journey' motif, beautifully realised in glass, stainless steel and bronze, permeates the building, creating an environment that encourages excellence through participation, guidance, discovery and achievement.

Within the pages of this book are many examples of Stephen's ability to combine spiritual and human values through his art. The effect is always positive, touching lives and inspiring hope. We are convinced that the superb training facilities of the CAPITAL BANK Foundation Building will continue to further this vision, helping individuals to succeed both in their business and their personal lives.

John Mercer, *Managing Director* CAPITAL BANK

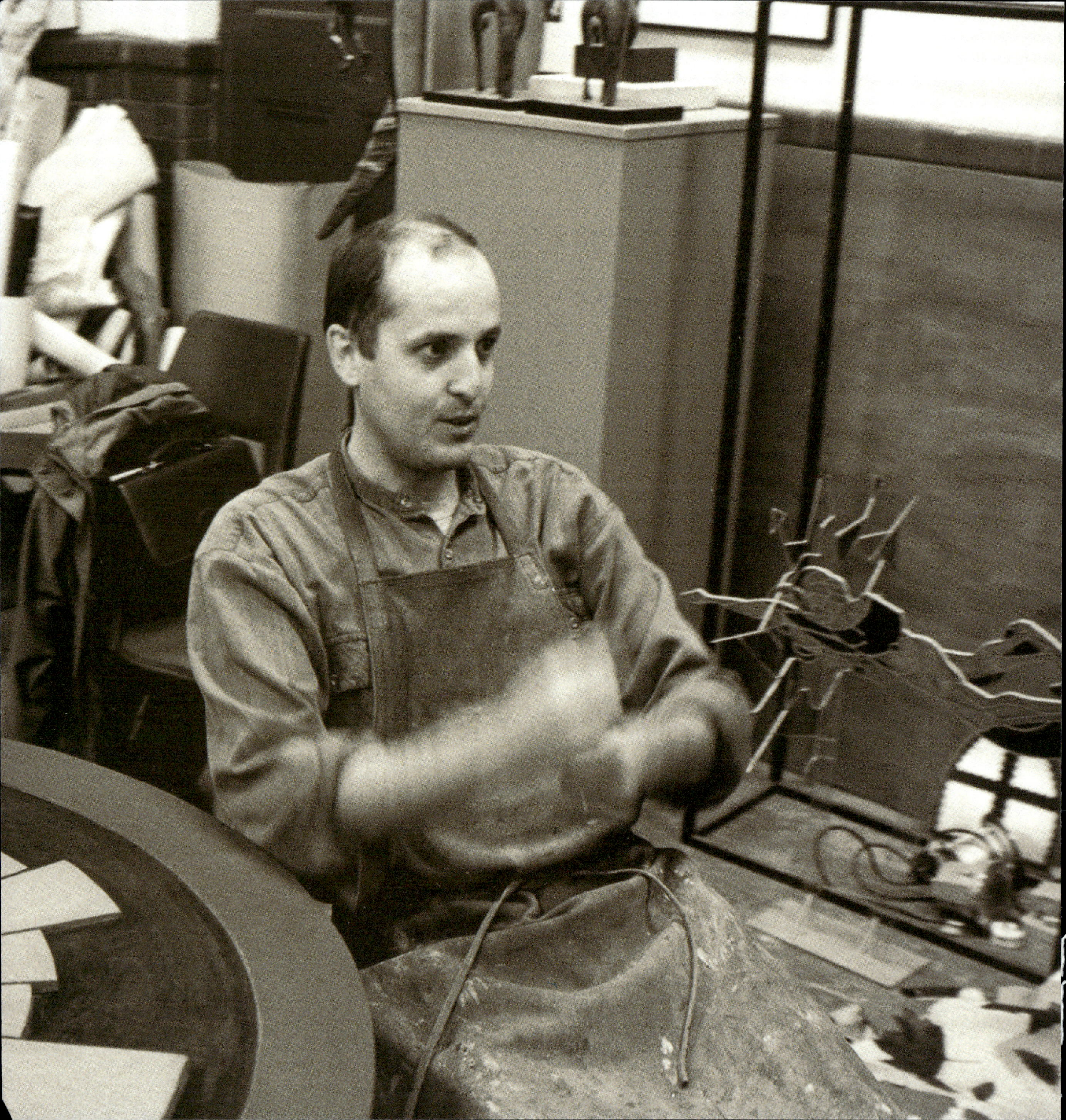

An Appreciation
by Stephen Smalley
Dean of Chester

Stephen Broadbent is a Christian Artist, whose work is becoming well established in this country. His first commissioned piece of sculpture, *Communication,* was for CAPITAL BANK in Chester. His other major work include *Reconciliation,* three imaginative figures in Glasgow, Liverpool and Belfast, and the exciting *Celebration of Chester* in the City's Town Hall Square. Stephen has recently sculpted a memorial walk-way in Warrington, and the outstanding *Water of Life* study, which is featured in this book, and was introduced in the Cloister Garden of Chester Cathedral in 1994.

Stephen's sensitivity and spirituality shine through his sculpture.

He is essentially a communicator, who works well with groups and individuals of all ages.

He is always impressively concerned that the communities with which he works should understand, and indeed own, the subjects which he sculpts; and this gives an important corporate dimension to his craftsmanship.

I commend this book most warmly to a wide readership.

About the Artist

Stephen Broadbent was born in Wroughton, Wiltshire in 1961. From an early age he intended to become a silversmith. However, it was through his association with the well known sculptor Arthur Dooley that he developed his affinity for sculpture. Stephen trained under Dooley in Liverpool, working initially with bronze and iron. He first exhibited in London in 1979, when he was 18 years old. Stephen, who lives in South Liverpool with his wife Lorraine, and their three children, Jed, Lucy and Isaac, works from the Bridewell Studios, Liverpool.

This book traces the major themes and ideas that have shaped the artist's work and beliefs, especially in the public domain where the power of his sculptures reach out and touch the lives of ordinary people.

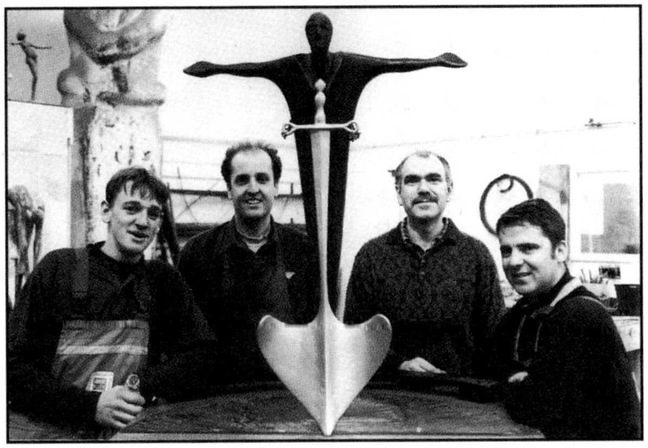

Contents

For many of us, art and art theory are vexing, mystifying subjects. Works of art do not yield up their meanings quickly. The language used to describe their unfamiliar forms is itself difficult, leaving the untutored viewer baffled and perplexed. Art appreciation is, it appears, a private world, inhabited by an educated elite. Why should this situation exist? One problem is that, unlike plumbers, postmen, carpenters and engineers, artists have become detached from the mainstream of our society. To many, what they do appears to engage with something that lies beyond ordinary experience. Also, their work does not attract investment in the same way that a project with defined utilitarian aims might. So as society invests in and manages practical pursuits, artists are largely left to fend for themselves. Yet when art is relegated to a ghetto with its own private language and an elitist appeal, almost everyone is left impoverished. Collectors and a coterie of artists may make a 'killing' through buying into the sub-culture. However, the majority of artists will have to put up with life in the margins as they struggle to realise their ideas without the resources required to bring them to fruition.

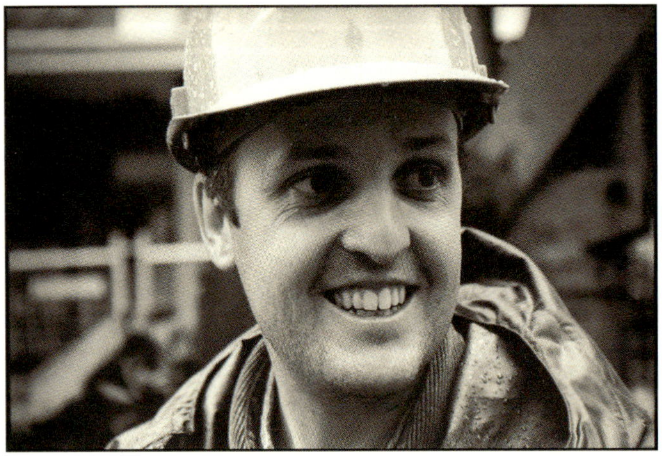

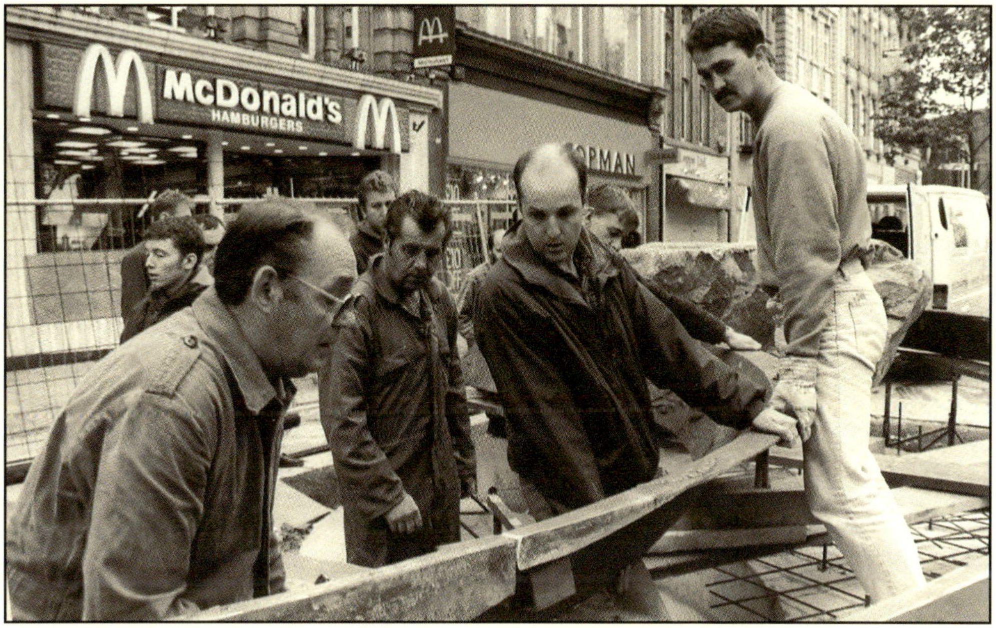

Art for art's sake?

To this can be added the self-regarding heritage of modernism. Indifferent to the viewer, contemptuous of materials, dismissive of artisanship, modernism has promoted a belief that the 'idea' is all. Little wonder then that for the man in the street, modern art looks unwilling to reach out and communicate. For the sculptor Stephen Broadbent, art has no right to this special status, cut off from the mainstream and from history, effectively an end in itself. He would prefer to place the viewer centre-stage, believing his work should act as a conduit to their feelings and emotions.

Restoring dignity to public art.

The audience he really seeks to communicate with is to be found not among the invited audience of the private gallery, but in the streets and squares of public places. Nowadays, craft and artisanship are spurned by many art lovers, who regard even the terms themselves as unfashionable and unsophisticated. Restoring the dignity of these skills has become a key motivation in Stephen Broadbent's work. This is achieved by allowing people in the community to participate in the physical processes that are involved in translating a concept into bronze, steel, iron or glass. These procedures demand skills that are found among people from all walks of life, many of whom will, if asked, deny having any formal knowledge of art. As they become involved in a project however, their appreciation of craft skills turns into appreciation of art. In this way the inspiration for the work is effectively returned to, and shared by the people for whom it was intended. This fulfils one of Broadbent's key aims, namely to make art as accessible as any other daily activity, thereby opening a door to understanding, enrichment and shared meaning.

Hope for the future

As the twentieth century draws to a close, the art of the western world continues to underline that for modern man, life is lived in a perpetual state of crisis, isolation and anxiety. It is therefore highly unusual, and somewhat unfashionable to discover a body of work by a living artist that reflects a sense of genuine faith in the future of people and their communities. Work that seeks a spiritual connection between art and the business of living, with all its crises and problems. Such is the work of the sculptor, Stephen Broadbent.

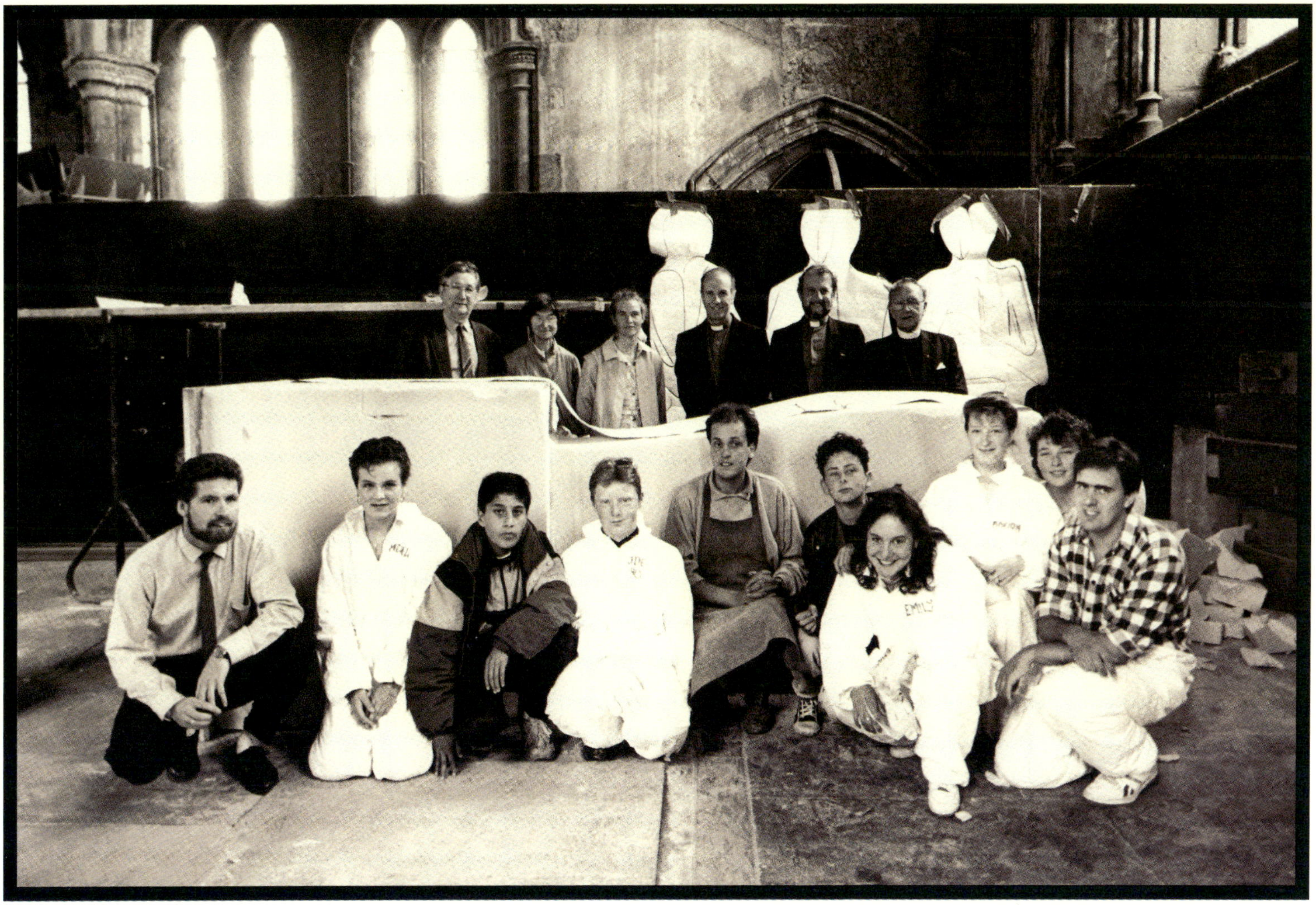

The artist pictured in Belfast with the whole cross-section of helpers and volunteers who co-operated in the Reconciliation project in 1989

THE CAPITAL BANK FOUNDATION - A JOURNEY

"Of the foundations and the building up
Of a Human Spirit thou has dared to tell
What may be told, to the understanding mind."
SAMUEL TAYLOR COLERIDGE
FROM: *to William Wordsworth,* COMPOSED ON THE NIGHT AFTER HIS RECITATION OF A POEM ON THE GROWTH OF THE INDIVIDUAL MIND.

"As iron sharpens iron, so one man sharpens another."
PROVERBS 27:17

The CAPITAL BANK Training Centre was built to facilitate a wide range of training initiatives from personal development, to team-building, and presentation skills. This purpose-designed building is now recognised as a Centre of Training Excellence in its own right.

The Foundation Building, commissioned by CAPITAL BANK is a tribute to the skills and imagination of its designers. An imaginative blend of traditional and modern materials and a light, airy environment make it the ideal venue for training and developing people.

Yet the Foundation Building is far more than a conventional, well-designed structure. It is the product of a unique partnership of art and practicality, made possible through co-operation and a willingness to accept the challenge of the new. In fact its very existence is a reminder of what it means to learn and grow.

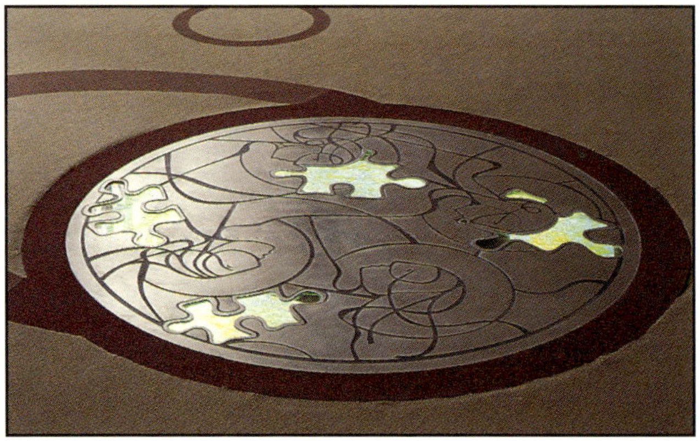

A journey of self-discovery

Once inside the unique CAPITAL BANK Foundation Building it is easy to appreciate why it is so different to all other training buildings

For, unlike these, its design is really a metaphor for the voyages of discovery we undertake as individuals at various stages of our lives. Although these journeys are all to do with learning, they are not embarked upon solely through books and formal education.

More often they take the form of disclosures, discoveries and moments of realisation. A steady, inevitable movement towards personal development, excellence, and hopefully, wisdom.

Nowhere is this sense of a journey better illustrated than in Broadbent's designs that were specially commissioned for the Foundation Building.

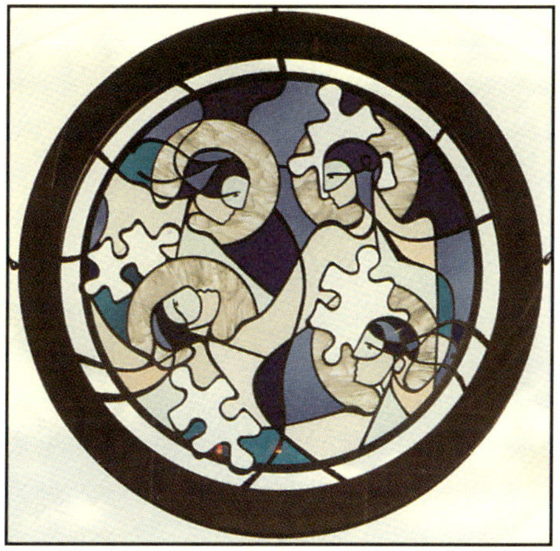

For the visitor the journey experience begins just beyond the building's threshold. The precise starting point is marked by a circular foundation stone, a feature that reflects CAPITAL BANK's heritage, Into this are etched the CAPITAL BANK logo in stainless steel, together with the name of its first managing director and the founding date. The stone is lit by fibre optic lights set into locally quarried sandstone pavings.

Above the foundation stone and pathway design hangs a welcoming medal entitled 'The Apprentices' - four figures interlocked within missing jigsaw pieces. Visitors proceed through revolving doors into the reception area, where a decorated floor medal containing the missing pieces is found. This provides the visitor with an intimation of experiences to come.

The missing pieces in the two-metre wide mosaic are disclosed via illumination from below.

These missing pieces suggest discovery, and clues to their meaning are found within the four corner designs. CAPITAL BANK's four founding principles: 'Vision', 'Challenge', 'Focus', and 'Achieve' complete the artwork in this area, realised through four stainless steel designs situated at the four 'corners' of the reception. Suspended above, the brilliantly coloured journeyman figures create a tranquil, cathedral-like atmosphere, rather like a stained glass window, giving natural light by day, and soft, interior illumination by night.

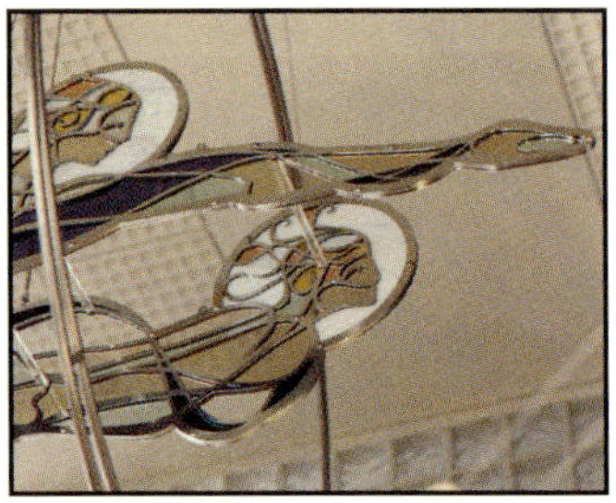

Moments of epiphany

These designs in steel and coloured glass were produced by employing a unique process that combines the ancient craft of stained glass making with advanced laser cutting technology whereby the glass is encapsulated with stainless steel rather than lead. The 'Journeymen' beckon the trainees onward, to further discoveries and greater achievements.

The idea of a journey of discovery is further emphasised in the atrium, a social area ablaze with colour from parallel rows of suspended decorative glass-patterned beams. The beams, which act as a colour filter for natural light as it enters from above are enhanced by a swirling, vividly coloured glass design that climaxes in a burst of colour and light as though in a flash of epiphany or enlightenment.

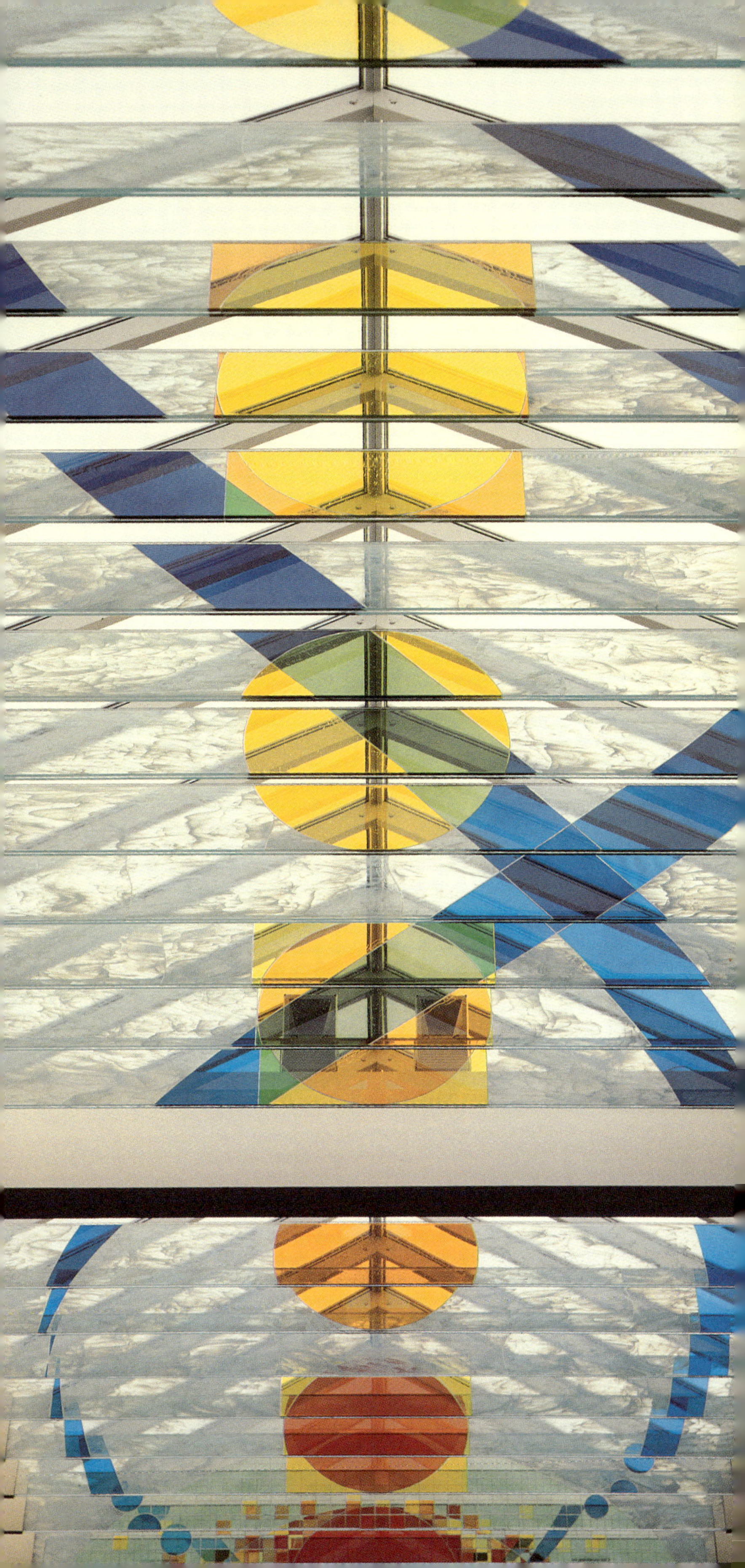

The Capital Bank Foundation - A Journey

As they mingle in the atrium, away from the functionality of the adjacent training rooms, the figures of visitors are bathed in the soft iridescence of reflected light.

Journey's end is marked by the Wrexham Road entrance where the two 'Master Craftsmen' bronzes hang as a permanent reminder of the achievements of the trainees who, beginning as 'apprentices', will hopefully progress to become 'journeymen' and finally 'master craftsmen' in their own right.

As well as enjoying the designs and sculptures of Stephen Broadbent, visitors will find the Foundation Building well endowed with artwork of all kinds from art students at the Blacon Arts Centre, Chester.

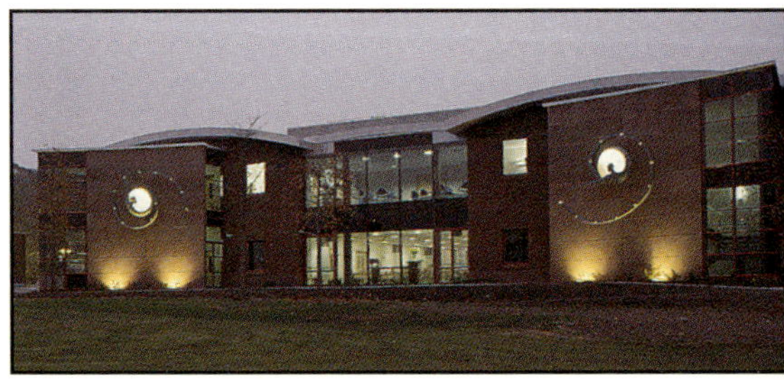

CAPITAL BANK donated £2,000 to the Centre to be spent on providing students with materials. Students then produced their interpretation of the Foundation theme, and from these CAPITAL BANK selected and purchased work which now hangs in the building.

John Mercer at the Bridewell Studios

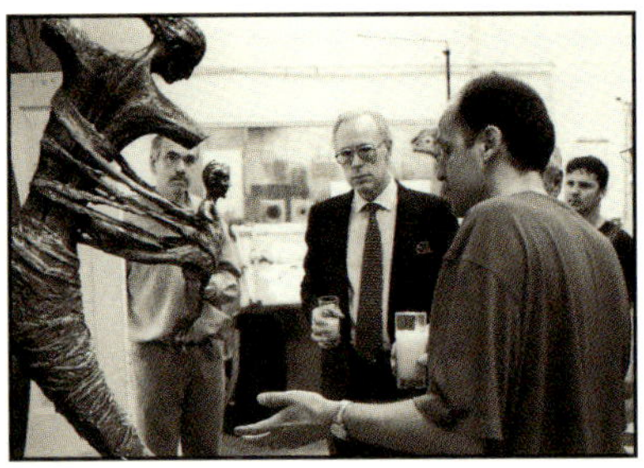

Broadbent wanted his designs to enhance the building while providing a fitting metaphor for its purpose. His thought processes led to the concept of the 'journey'.

His proposals were readily accepted by CAPITAL BANK, and after presenting an outline scheme to the directors he was commissioned to produce a number of maquettes. The first, 'The End of the Journey', was followed by the major pieces representing each symbolic stage of the journey.

Although he was given the freedom he needed, Broadbent knew from previous experience that the art of 'making it happen' would prove to be just as important as creating the work itself, and that his presence on site would be both a threat and an opportunity for everyone involved in the project.

An artist on site

In a world where the word of the professional architect generally goes unchallenged, the presence of an unpredictable sculptor on site can be perceived as an unnecessary extravagance, even an irritation.

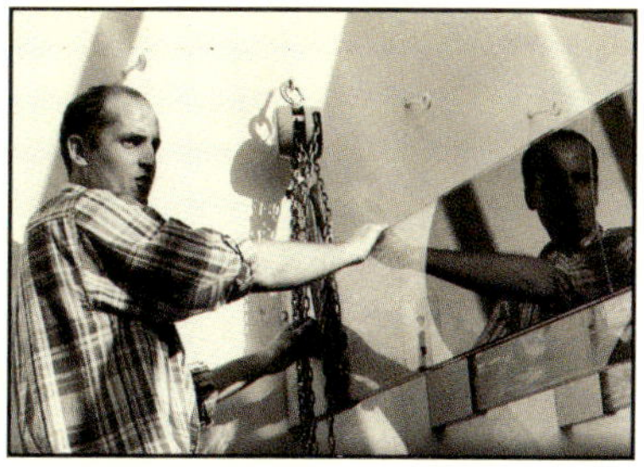

How, for example would the artist cement a working relationship with the design-build professionals? How willing would they be to work with the pure aesthetic of sculpture? Would it be possible to marry the tried and tested methods of system-building and modular design with the concepts of high art?

For him this was an extension of the journey in the sense that the success of the project was partly dependent upon inter-action, the testing and frank evaluation of artistic concepts by a public not renowned for its tact or diplomacy. This was the real world beyond the studio. A place where art needed to connect with the hard-nosed practicalities of the commercial world. It was a challenge made all the more acute by the timing of Broadbent's entry.

THE CAPITAL BANK FOUNDATION - A JOURNEY

The Foundation Building was to give him the opportunity to become not only artist, but artistic liaison officer. A person who simultaneously creates, facilitates and co-ordinates.

For Broadbent, this is how it should be. Living art encompasses far more than the creative act or idea. It means being willing to communicate with others, to acknowledge their ideas, and to work with them to overcome problems.

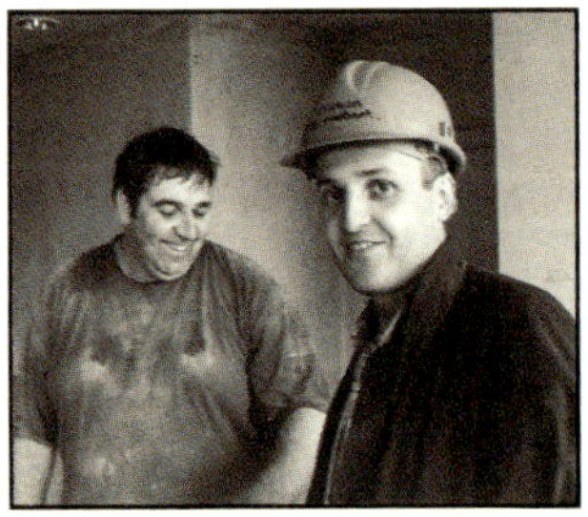

And, one of the most satisfying features of the Foundation Building is that its success owes so much to the application of the principles of learning and co-operation it was created to foster.

A place apart

There is also a sense in which the Foundation Building symbolises the ability of the artist to interpret the need of the individual for a 'place apart', with its own unique atmosphere.

An environment completely different to any other that might exist in the CAPITAL BANK organisation. Inside, visitors will find little trace of the traditional office environment. Instead they will discover a place where ideas and people can develop, free from the distractions of corporate life.

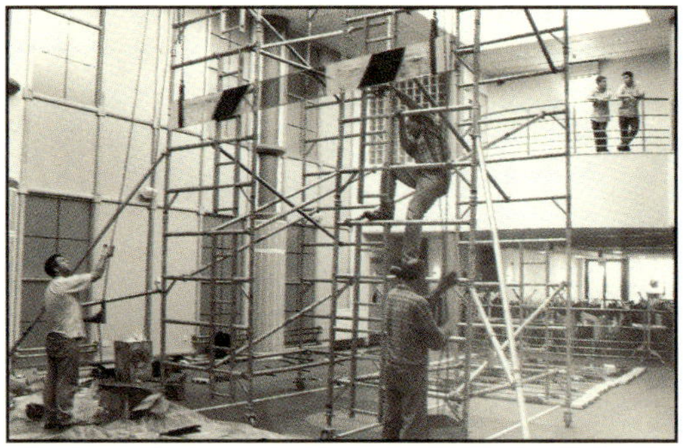

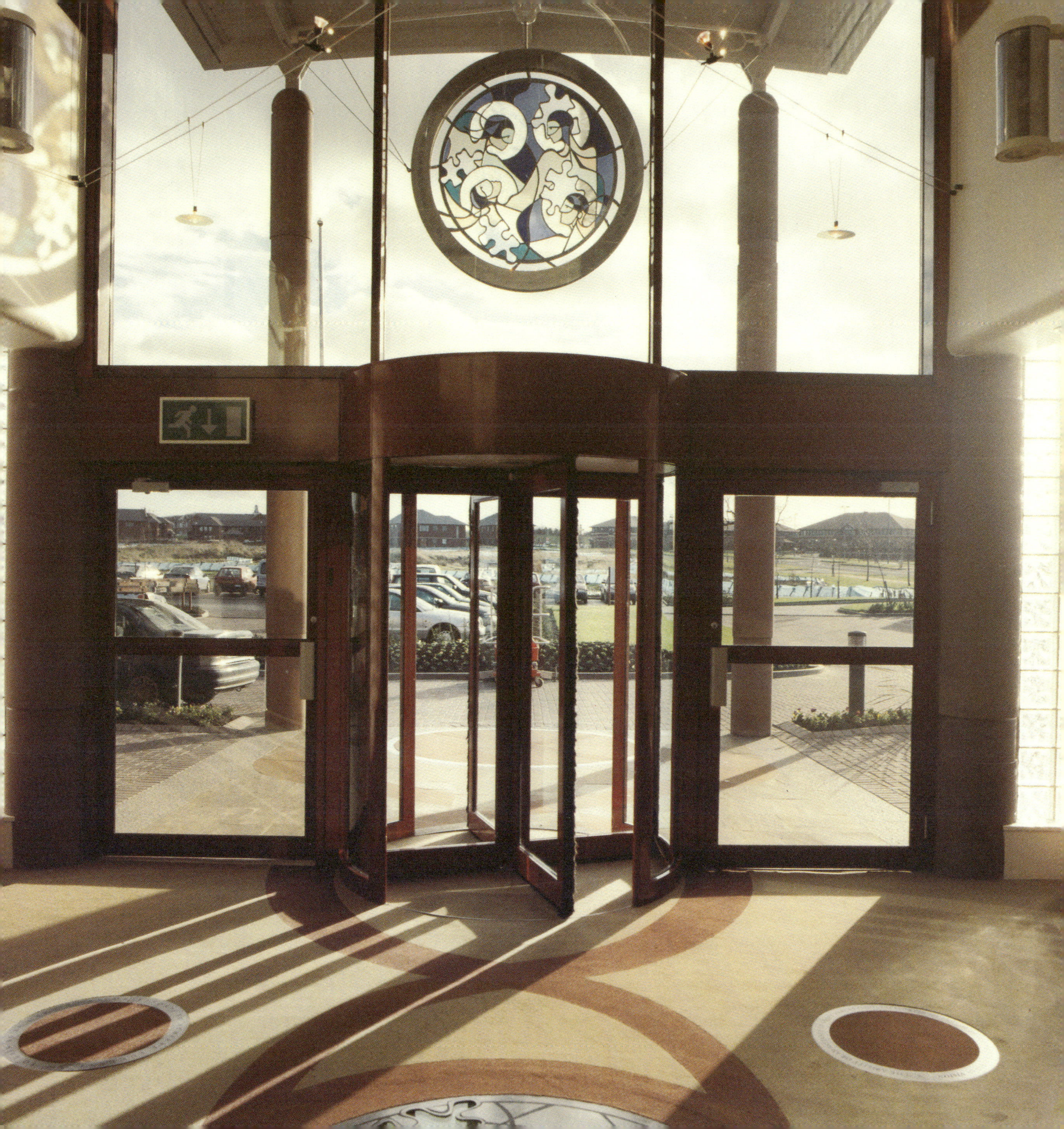

There is a sense in which all displayed art can be described as public art. After all, art galleries are public places, open to everyone, regardless of their position or social status.

In this sense, access to beautiful artefacts is a democratic right. Yet still, the language of art appreciation is not universal. Its semantic codes are not readily understood by 'the public', and genuine critical responses, even to public works, remains the prerogative of the educated few.

The open-air studio erected for the celebration of Chester Sculpture

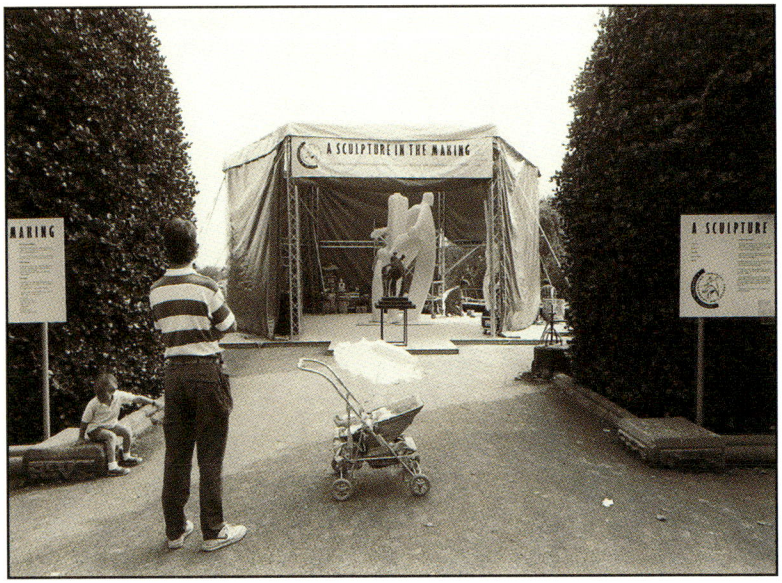

Public or community artist?

So is Stephen Broadbent's commitment to public art a mission to redress the balance? A partial answer to this question can be found in the distinctions that may be drawn between public and community art.

Community art is, by definition 'people', rather than 'art' - oriented. Although, on occasion, the work Broadbent does certainly involves people in the making process, his work is not bounded by the limitations that affect the community artist.

The need for artistic control

Community artists act as facilitators. Their role is to allow people to discover and create their own art, a process which, to succeed, demands a gradual retreat on the part of the artist as the confidence of the participants grows.

Although the benefits of community art are unquestionable, its ends are clearly different to those of public art. With community art the value is in the making. The people who become involved are exposed to new experiences, discovering talents yet to be developed. As a result, worthy though the end product may be, it is in a sense ephemeral, a 'snapshot' which is unlikely to be strong enough to stand the tests placed upon a permanent, sited work of art. In this sense community art is governed by a completely different set of values to those of public art.

The work of John Varley's iron foundry St Helens

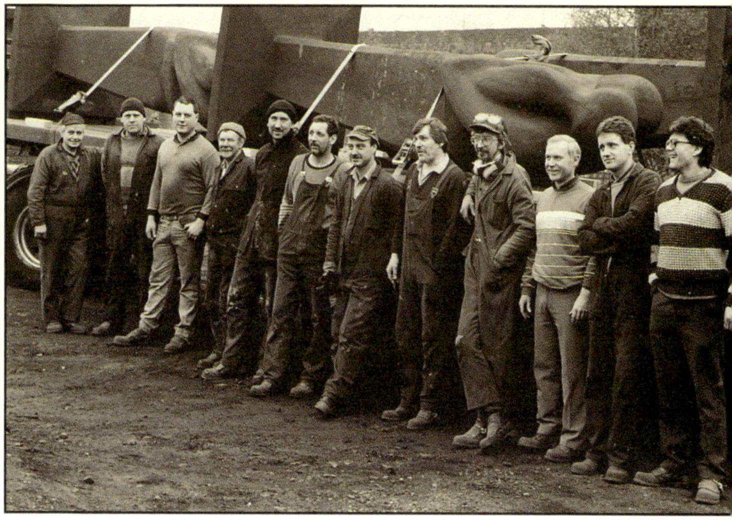

Seen in this light, Stephen Broadbent is not a community artist. Rather he is a public artist who has a particular attitude towards the public and the community at large.

In his view, the artist must take overall control if the work of art is to achieve a permanent and symbolic status within the community. Yet the work itself is produced with a human dimension that is designed to strike a chord with, and hopefully to serve the needs of the community.

The legacy of modernism

Thirty years ago the idea of public art as a medium for communication with the public would have been regarded as absurd. The modernist preoccupation with form had created an aesthetic totally disengaged from the human and social sphere.

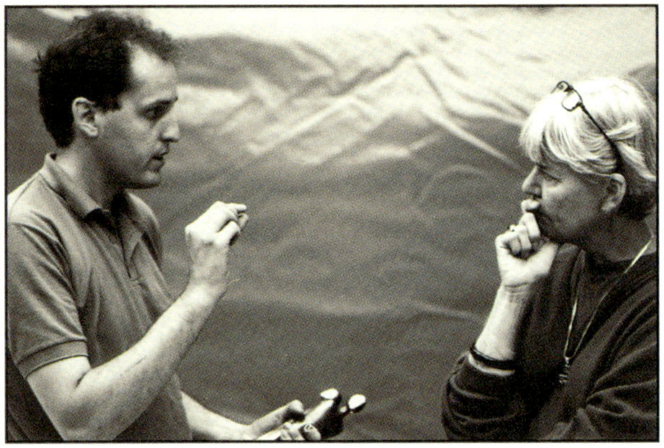

The end product, still very much in evidence in contemporary culture, is a form of art as alienation, a self-regarding process where form is exalted above human and social concerns.

This triumph of the abstract over the human is nowhere more evident than in our towns and city centres, many of which are completely bereft of any visual stimuli to which people can relate.

Post-modernism merely complicates the problem by taking the cultural and religious icons of the past and juxtaposing them with the transient symbols of our own rapidly changing times.

In recognition of this, some artists moved their galleries into the public arena. However in doing so they simply moved the complexity of the situation to a new location. The fact remained that artists, although conscious of the need to expose the public to their work, were still working essentially for a specialist audience, an educated coterie.

For Stephen Broadbent the answer to this problem lies in the development of public art. In the open environment of the city street, the artist can claim a genuine daily connection between the artefact and the community.

Yet it is not an easy task. The problems facing the public artist working in this environment are vastly more complex than those of his predecessors.

Seeking universal symbols

Our cities are no longer places that accurately reflect settled civic values. In an increasingly secular age, racked by uncertainty and loss of faith, univocal symbols that speak directly to all are few and far between. Creating a symbol around which the common heritage and shared aspirations of a city or community can cluster is an extraordinarily difficult challenge.

Post-modernism has taught us that history is not a continuum into which we are accommodated, but a kind of store of memorabilia which can be raided at will to decorate the present.

In our world, declining spiritual values and a sense of crisis and uncertainty about our identity have replaced the old certainties as society becomes increasingly fragmented and complex.

Despite the fact that the 'world view' of most people is no longer dictated by religious imperatives, the dedicated public artist cannot retreat into the world of pure aesthetics, but must instead strive to 'square the circle'. He is forced to engage with the social dimension head on.

To set about rediscovering the values and potentials that can unite people, reinterpreting them symbolically. In the world of public art, however, good creative ideas can often be stifled by civic and political concerns. It is a problem that the public artist must tackle, with a mixture of co-operation, tact and diplomacy to ensure that his projects not only see the light of day, but are also well received. These skills go beyond art and design and into the world of human relationships. They involve dealing with people and making things happen, sometimes against the odds.

In the field of public art, the Art Administrator is often perceived as the person who imparts the vision to the artist who then interprets it. Broadbent argues that in the realm of public art, it is the artist who should take control of these issues. Where a need exists, it is up to the artist to seize the moment, rather than waiting for a commission to arrive. He should make the first move, drawing up and presenting suggestions, making models, visualising his ideas for others. Sometimes the original idea may come from the patron. This, coupled with the imagination of the artist can inspire others to visualise and back a grand and exciting scheme out of all proportion to that originally envisaged. The artist's role is to create the idea, to feed and develop it, to inspire the onlookers. In this sense, he can accomplish more than the merely architectural, enabling vision to triumph over the practical.

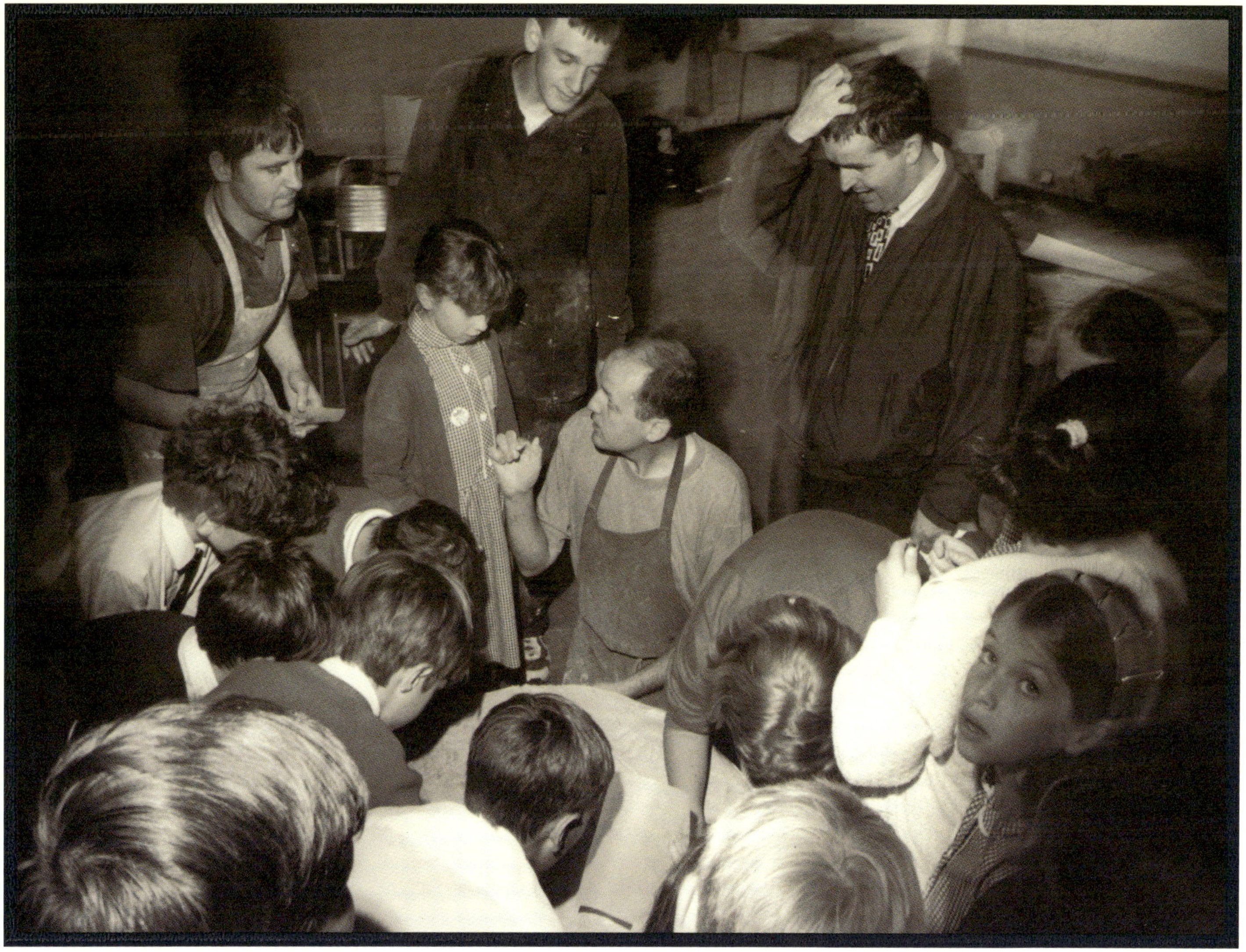

School children of Warrington developing ideas for the pavement disks installed on the Bridge Street River of Life design

1994

WARRINGTON - THE RIVER OF LIFE

The 'River of Life' at Upper Bridge Street, Warrington was commissioned in the aftermath of the 1993 IRA bomb which killed two young boys, injured dozens of citizens and shocked the sensibilities of people the world over.

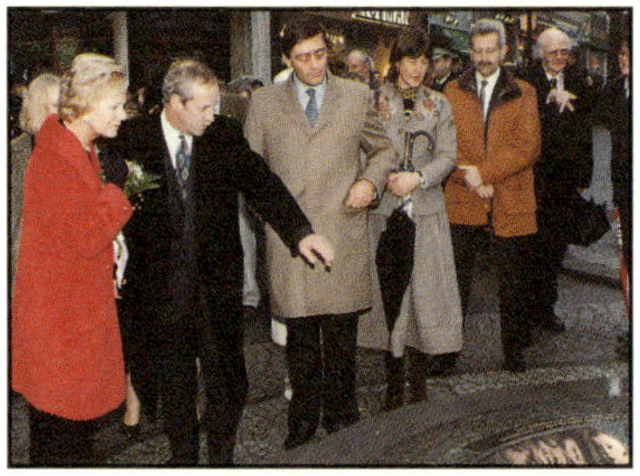

The re-development was formally opened on 14 November 1996 by Her Royal Highness the Duchess of Kent. The event was also attended by family members of the two boys who died in the bombing and other members of the community who were deeply affected by the tragedy.

A catalyst for renewal

The project was not, however, undertaken solely in response to the bombing. It also fitted in with one of the eight strategic objectives for Warrington, namely "to enhance the town centre's attractiveness through animation, Public Art features, and play facilities which reflect community ownership and civic pride." For some years, Warrington Borough Council had been planning major changes to breathe new life back into the town centre. The 1993 bomb added new urgency to these plans, and in 1994 the Council began to implement its renewal strategy. The 'River Of Life' project gave the town an opportunity to create a permanent memorial to the victims of the IRA bomb.

'Then the angel showed me the river of the water of life, as clear as crystal, flowing out from the throne of God and of the Lamb down the middle of the great street of the city. On each side of the river stood the tree of life, bearing twelve crops of fruit, yielding its fruit every month. And the leaves of the tree are here for the healing of the nations. No longer will there be any curse.'

REVELATION 22:1 -3

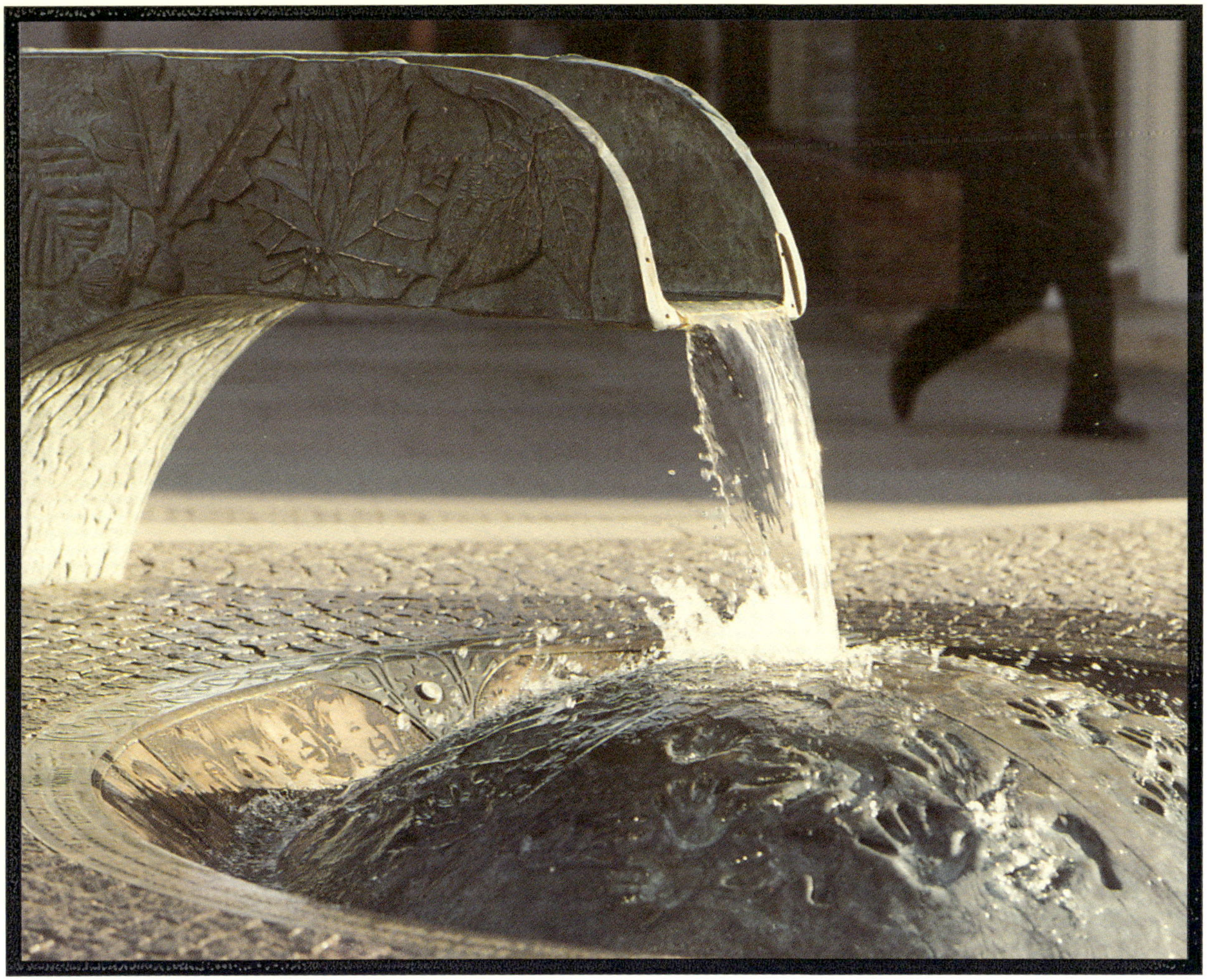

The literal and spiritual significance of water is explored through the 'River of Life'

Yet throughout the community opinion was divided as to whether this should be done.

A fitting memorial

Many people felt that it was better to allow time to heal the wounds that had been inflicted. Others needed a focus for their grief and somehow make sense of the suffering. For them a formal remembrance was essential.

In a way, the scheme answered both these needs. It provided an opportunity to create a complete town centre street re-development incorporating leisure, and play facilities. An environment designed for the enjoyment and benefit of the whole community.

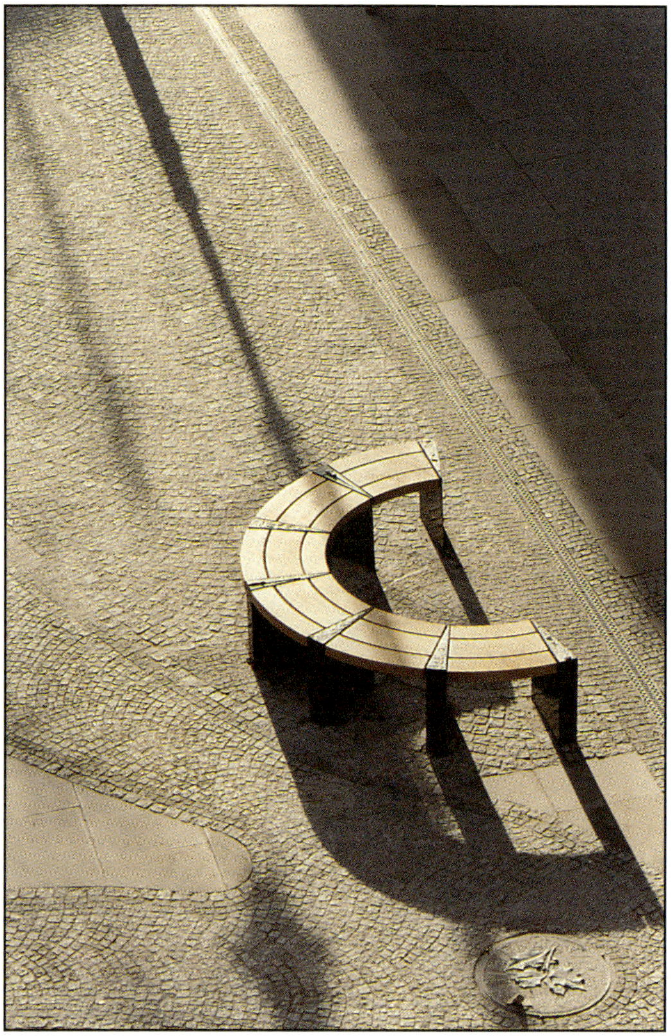

The development itself became, not a stark memorial in an unaltered landscape, but a symbol of renewal and faith in the power of the human spirit to triumph over adversity and to invest the future with hope.

Water - a symbol of healing

River of Life draws its inspiration from the powerful description of waters 'for the healing of the nations' described in the book of Revelation.

This symbolic, water source is re-created over the full length of the pedestrianised section of Upper Bridge Street, climaxing in a raised water feature that literally springs forth from its centre.

Water, both in its literal and symbolic forms, is the key to the sculpture. It is the tears shed by victims of loss, but it is also a symbol of healing, of cleansing, and of renewal.

At the start the literal element flows river-like over a glacial boulder. This is more than a decorative effect however, since the boulder is intended as a metaphor for the broken body of Christ, who gave his life on behalf of the world of mankind.

The Alpha and the Omega

A closer look reveals the letter alpha inscribed in the boulder thus marking the beginning both of a natural and a spiritual cycle, and echoing the words "I am the alpha and the omega" that were uttered to the apostle John.

The water courses along a bronze channel before cascading onto a dome standing at the heart of the water feature. The dome, inscribed with the word 'omega' is a fitting symbol for the completion of both the natural and spiritual cycles.

The dome was originally made of putty in which children and the relatives of the bomb victims made hand imprints which were then cast in bronze. Now, the handprints are continually washed by water flowing from the boulder - a symbolic source of healing - on to the dome. In unconscious gestures of remembrance, children spontaneously put their hands into the water to find prints that match their own. Photographs of children, their faces etched in bronze, form a circle of companions around the bowl's interior, among them are bomb victims Jonathan Ball and Tim Parry.

The life-giving power of water

The decorative bronze work of the water feature dramatically recreates the Bible's account of creation from its beginning, as the spirit of God moves over the waters of the as yet unformed earth. In due course life, pictured by plants and wildlife springs from the river in all its profusion.

The theme is carried throughout the street-scape, including high quality English Oak bench seating crafted in a variety of shapes and sizes, and decorated in bronze using images that reflected the town's rich industrial heritage.

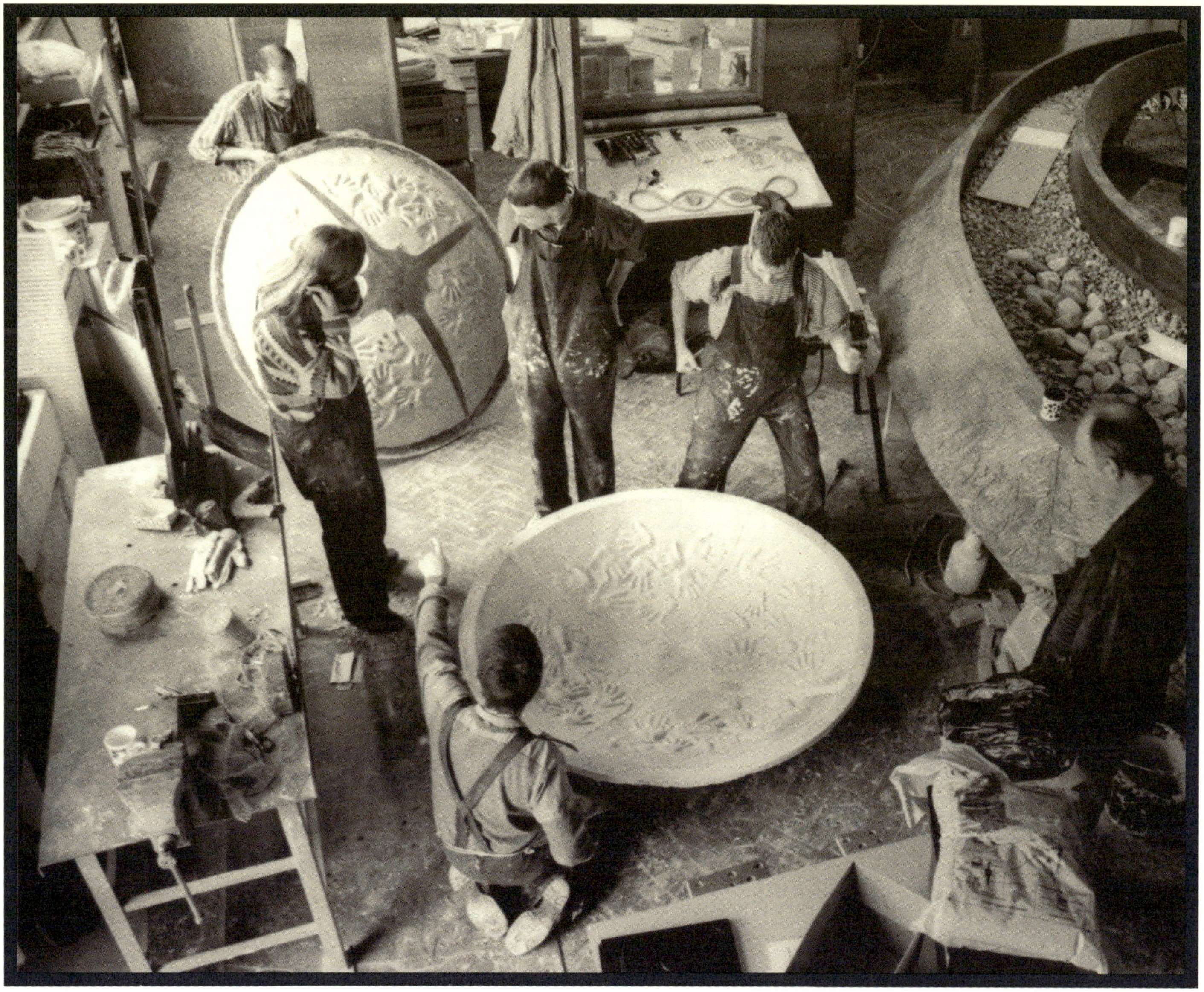

New lighting, also designed by the artist has helped to transform the street. Low-level lamps have been introduced which enhance the daytime street-scape, and add ambience to the night scene, shedding pools of soft light. Appropriately, angels look down from the cast metal designs of the lamp posts. With its historical associations of continuity, wealth, and prosperity The River Mersey was the ideal counterpoint for the River of Life theme.

Using natural stone and granite sets, Broadbent's team worked in all weathers, mapping out a design that accurately mirrors the meandering course of the river as it passes through the borough of Warrington.

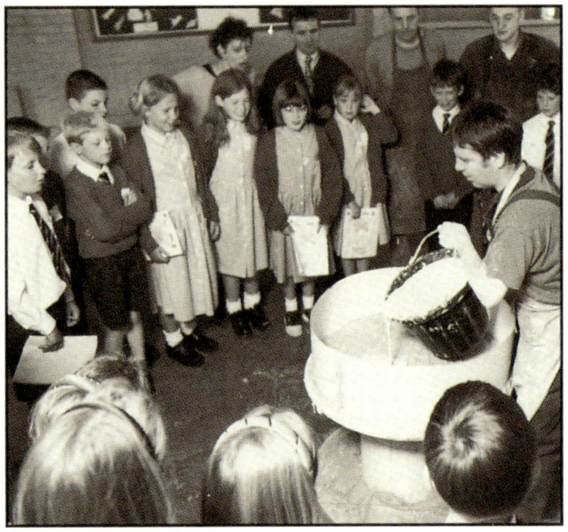

The contribution of children

Twelve bronze discs are also set into the pavement at intervals along the length of the 'river'. The artwork was prepared by pupils from 12 local schools, and their designs blend elements of the Revelation vision with everyday features of the children's lives.

The background of each disc is a section of an ordnance survey map depicting the immediate area around the school overlaid with images of Warrington past and present, specially drawn by the pupils.

The children were asked to select 12 different leaves and fruits. These are foregrounded on each disc along with their name, the name of the month of the year, and that of the individual school. Within the design, the literal fruits modulate into the fruitage of positive human relationships, reflecting qualities of reconciliation, joy, healing, forgiveness, justice, patience - symbols of faith and hope in uncertain times.

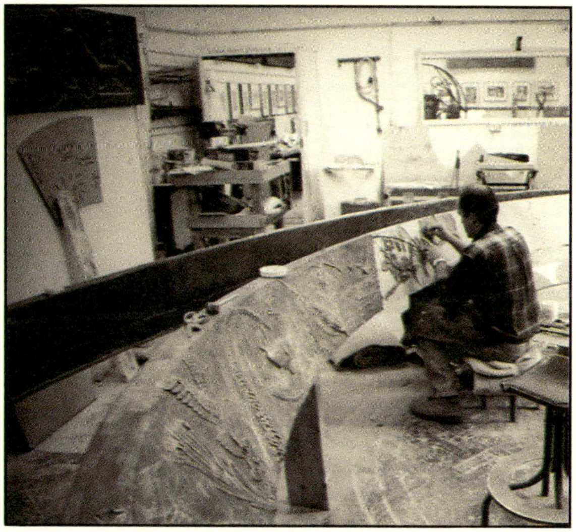

In this way the design echoes the symbolic meaning of the Revelation vision, re-working it and drawing strength from the certainty of its message.

The discs have undoubtedly made a major contribution to the success of the 'River of Life' project, providing children with a real opportunity to participate and learn. Originally, this important feature of the 'River of Life' was not covered by the original budget, and was only made possible by sponsorship from North West Water.

More than a work of art

At every level, the Upper Bridge Street development evokes the physical and spiritual associations of water and of the river as everlasting symbols of renewal, healing, growth and refreshment for individuals and communities.

The task was to create a complete environment that would serve as a celebration of Warrington and its past, and provide a place where people could meet, sit, talk and play.

The implications went much further than art however, reaching out to touch the life of the community itself. The creation in Warrington of a successful marriage of art and architecture has also benefited other artists interested in working in the public domain.

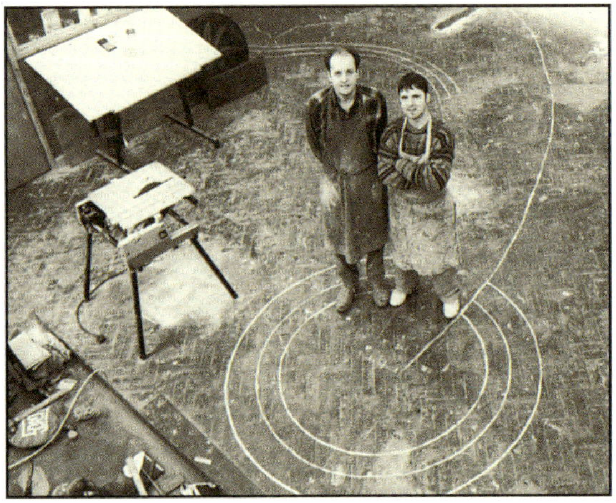

At the time the inclusion of a lead artist in an urban development team was a brave move for a Borough Council. Even though Broadbent's ideas led to the scrapping of the Council's plans for the town centre, to their credit, the town planners rose to the challenge.

In such a situation the artist's stress on the importance of the human dimension can at times lead to a conflict between artistic creativity and the brow-beating cynicism of town planners. At points in its three year development, the 'River of Life' project was occasionally to test the determination of Broadbent and his team to the limit. The main problem revolved around 'making things happen' in a culture where progress is driven largely by committee. Even though he was appointed Lead Artist, Broadbent often found himself frustrated by bureaucracy and red tape.

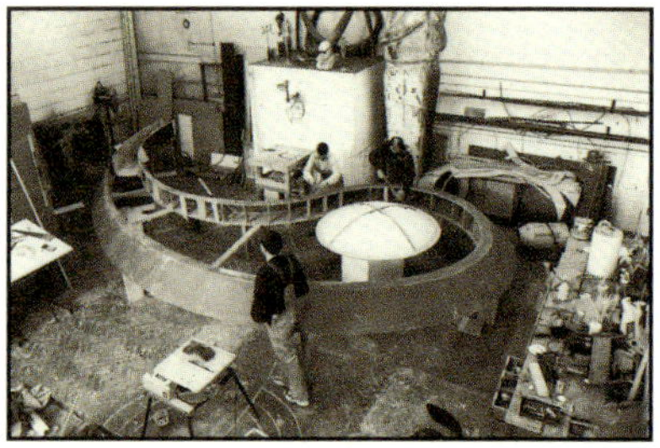

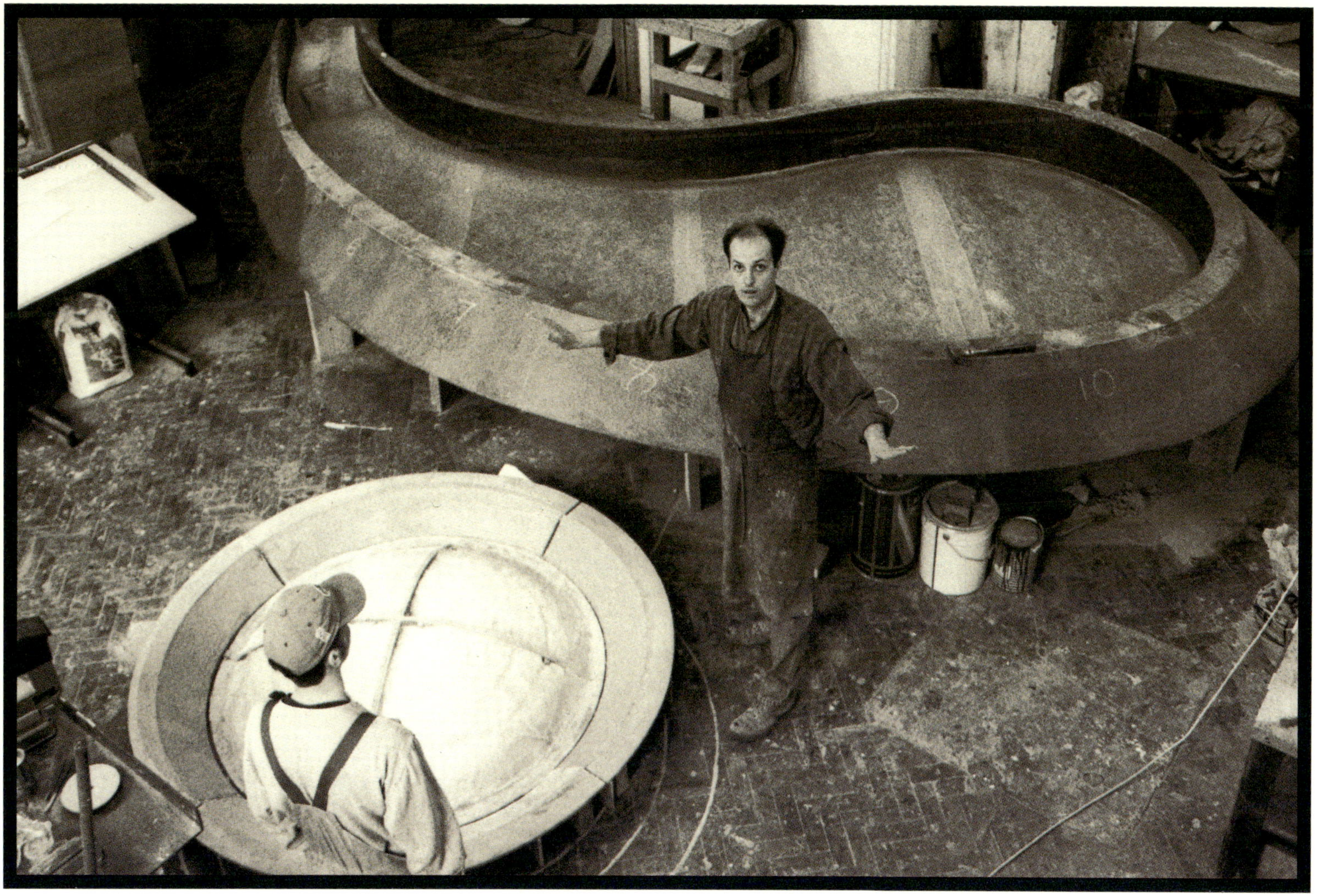

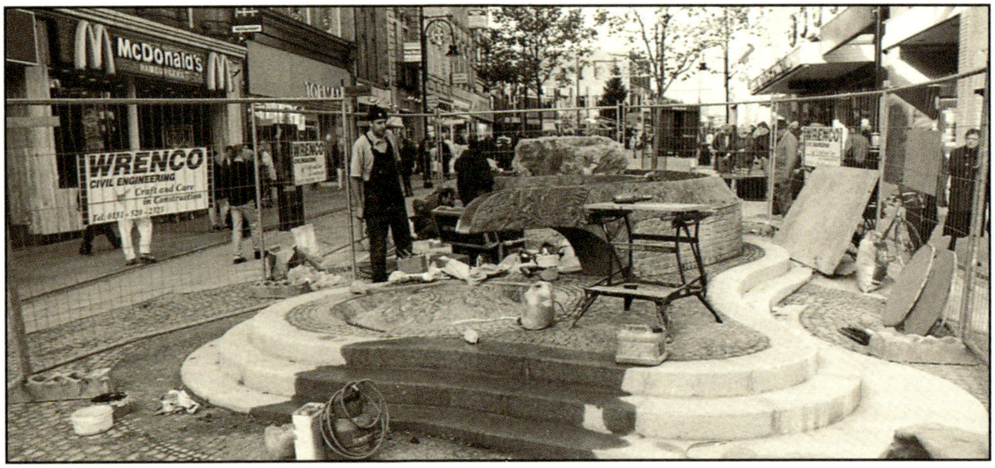

To some extent this was perfectly understandable. Broadbent's team needed to accommodate the complex needs of local politics while advocating and promoting an all-embracing concept that was largely outside the experience of town planners.

To add to the problem, there was in effect no municipal 'champion', or personality to drive the project forward, make decisions or take risks. The onus for this fell upon the artist, who found himself sandwiched between inspiration and practicality.

Yet somehow, despite all the difficulties and setbacks, the town centre project was a huge success. So what was it that drove it forward? Obviously a great deal of time and energy had been invested in the project.

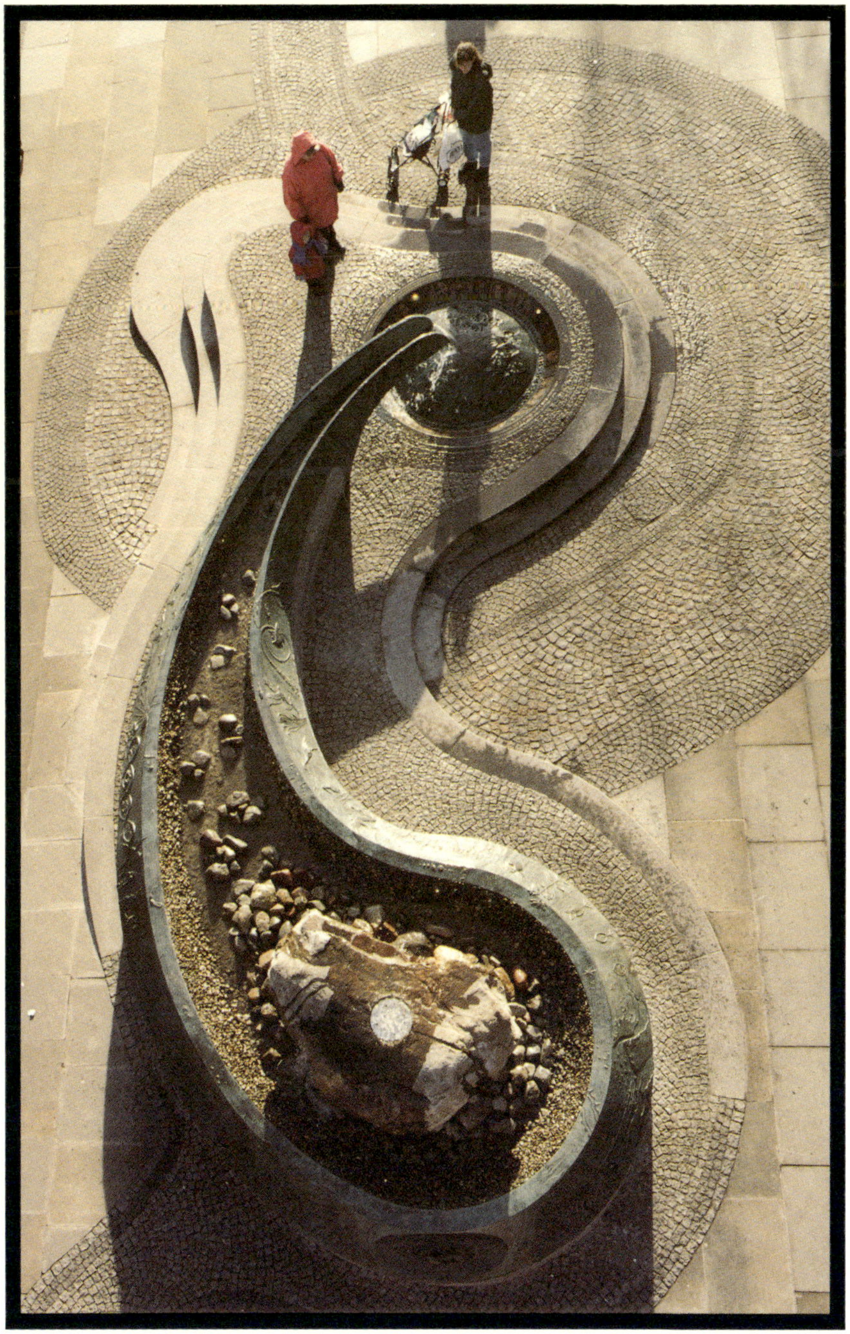

A powerful vision

However there were other, more important motivating factors. The families of the victims, especially the parents of Timothy Parry and the father of Jonathan Ball, were not concerned about bureaucracy or politics.

Their willingness to share the artist's vision, coupled with significant moral support from the community, as well as welcome financial support from the Duke of Westminster, transcended petty difficulties and powered the project through to its resoundingly successful conclusion.

Even now, with the benefit of hindsight, Stephen and his team have been unable to evaluate the impact of the Warrington experience.

One thing is clear however. The IRA bomb that exploded in Warrington in 1993 not only shattered the lives of its victims, it also acted as an agent of change that was felt at every level - personal, corporate, and civic.

Ironically, this single act of devastation set in motion a powerful counter-movement, an unstoppable force for good that undoubtedly helps to bring healing to the people of Warrington.

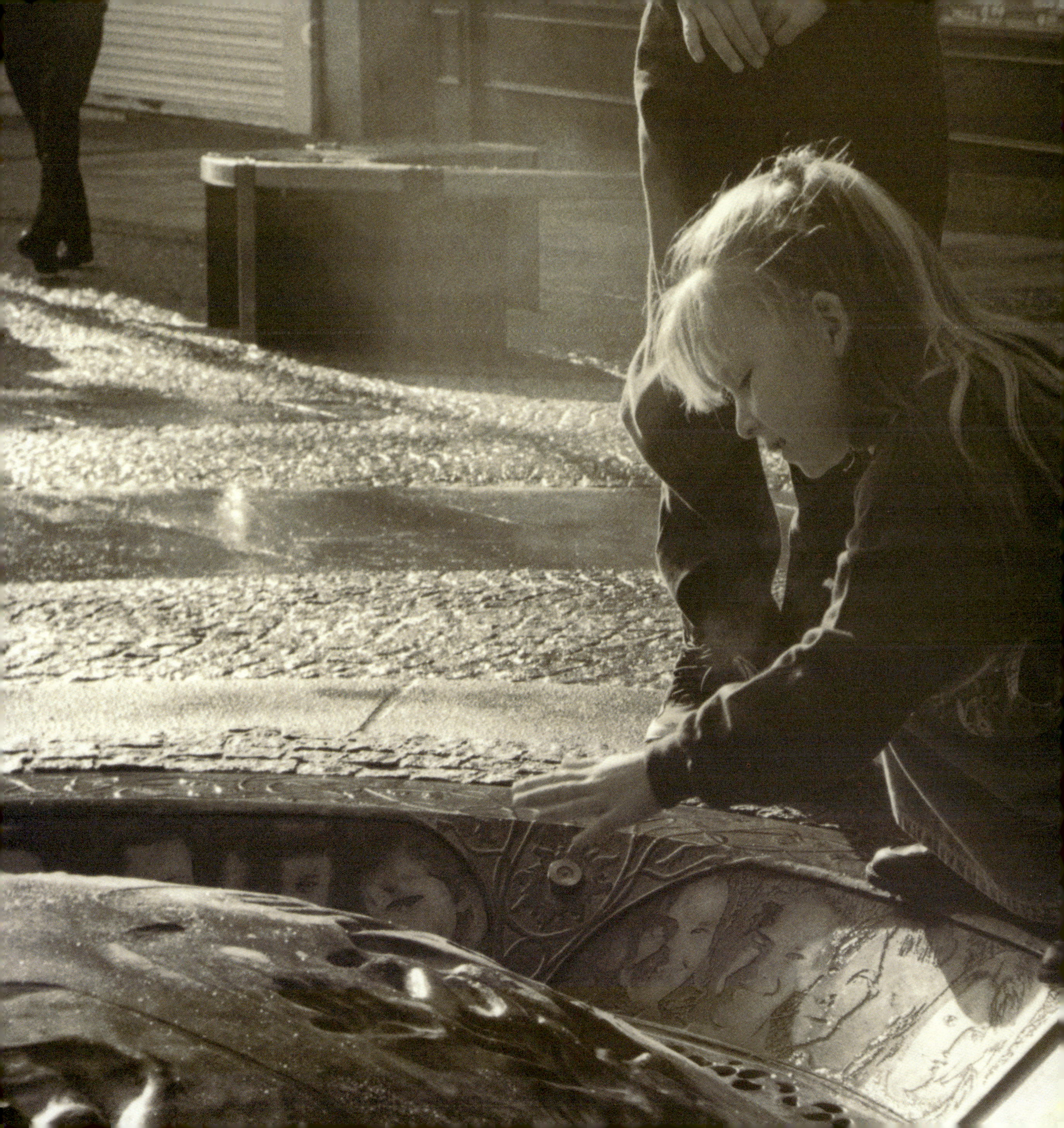

1994

Water of Life

"But the fruit of the Spirit is love, joy, peace, patience, kindness, goodness, faith, gentleness, self control. Against such things there is no law."
GALATIANS 5:22-23

This striking 10foot bronze sculpture, commissioned for the Cloister Gardens of Chester Cathedral is a beautiful work of art in its own right. However, its appeal extends far beyond the aesthetic.

Through its location in the centre of the Cloister Garden, on the site of the contemplative monks' original water source, 'Water of Life' appropriately complements the Cathedral's tranquil environment.

In answer Jesus said to her: "Everyone drinking from this water will get thirsty again, but whoever drinks the water that I give him will never thirst again. Indeed, the water I give him will become in him a spring of water welling up imparting everlasting life."
JOHN 4:13-14

More significantly, however, it provides a genuine focal point for meditation on the profound nature of spiritual experiences. The sculpture, gifted to the Cathedral by CAPITAL BANK plc, depicts the encounter between Jesus and the Woman of Samaria. It was introduced to the Cathedral to mark the 900th Anniversary of the foundation of the Benedictine Abbey of St Werburgh on the site in 1092.

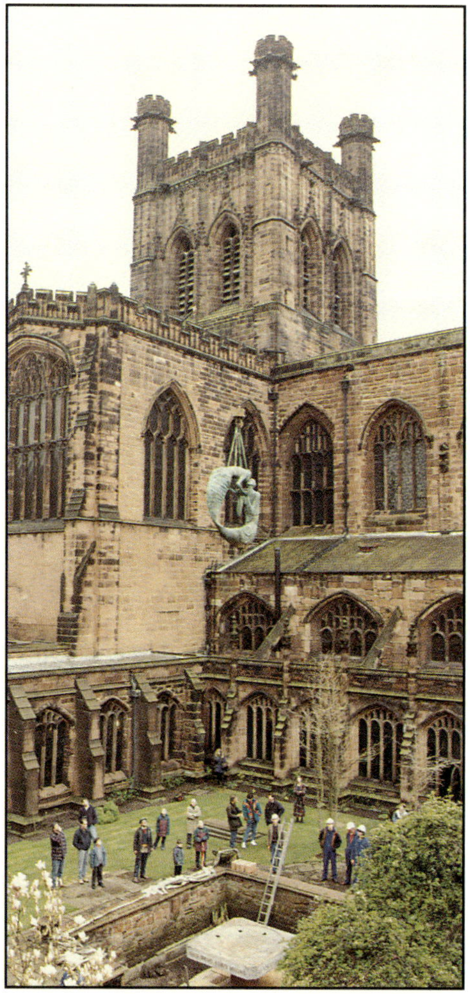

The 'Water of Life' sculpture is lowered into position

This is clearly an outstanding modern work of art, perhaps one of the most distinguished to be created for any English cathedral this century.

The sculpture is a brilliant representation of the meeting between Jesus and a Samaritan woman who was collecting water at Jacob's well, located just outside the city of Sychar, in what is now Palestine, or modern-day Israel. The Gospel account is a powerful illustration of the way one person's life was changed by a single encounter with the Son of God.

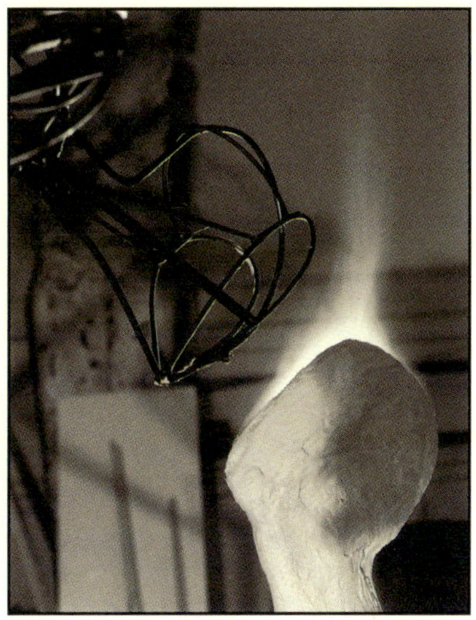

Half Jew and half Gentile, the Samaritan people lived in the 10 tribe northern kingdom prior to its conquest in 740 B.C.

With its chequered history, including invasion by Assyrian tribes, some Samaritans were undoubtedly the product of mixed marriages.

However in Jesus' day, the name carried a religious, rather than a racial connotation, referring to one who belonged to the religious sect that flourished in the vicinity of ancient Shechem, and who observed tenets distinctly different to those of Judaism.

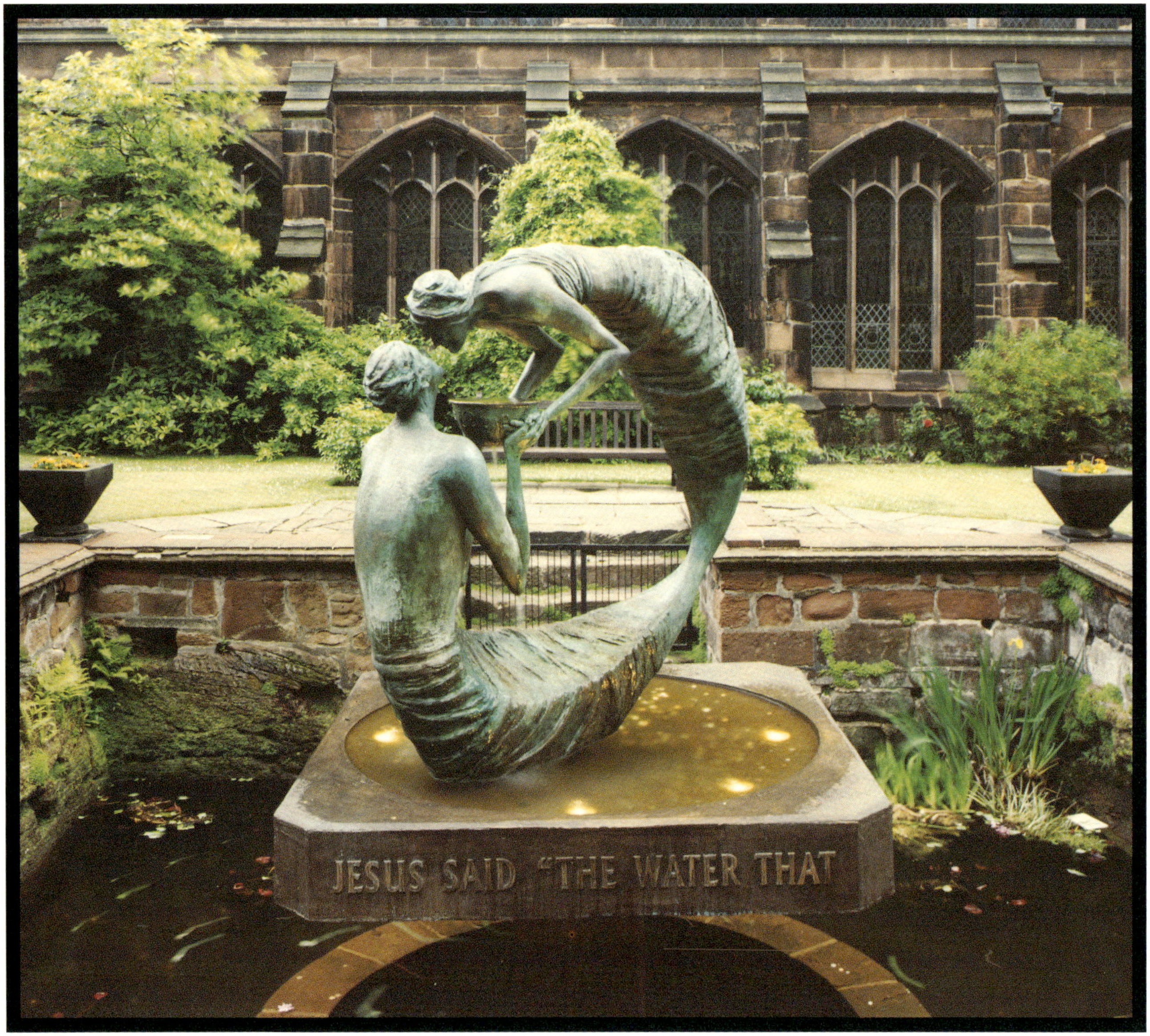
JESUS SAID "THE WATER THAT

Historically, Samaritans and Jews regarded one another with disdain, so it was all the more surprising that the woman at the well should converse with Jesus, let alone allow herself to be deeply influenced by him. By the time of her meeting with Jesus, she had married and divorced five times, and was living with a man without the benefit of marriage.

She came to the well at noon, the hottest time of the day, perhaps because of an emergency, perhaps out of shame, to avoid the crowds. Drawing closer, she saw Jesus sitting beside it, looking intently at her. After she has drawn water, he asks her for a drink. Taken aback, she replies, "How come that you, a Jew, ask a Samaritan woman for a drink?"

Jesus answers, "If you knew the gift of God, and who it is that is saying to you 'give me a drink', you would have asked him, and he would have given you living water."

Confused, the woman responds with the words, "Sir, you have no bucket, and the well is deep. Where do you get that living water?"

Jesus replies, "Everyone who drinks of this water will be thirsty again, but those who drink the water that I will give them will never get thirsty at all, because the water that I will give him will become within him a fountain of water bubbling up to impart everlasting life."

On hearing this she says immediately, "Sir, give me this water!" From that moment on, the woman's whole course of life is completely changed.

The Water of Life Sculpture explores the literal and spiritual life-giving properties of water. The circular shape brings the protagonists face-to-face, lending intensity and tenderness to the encounter, in itself an act of simple human kindness.

The viewer, confronted with water, both literal and figurative, brimming endlessly from the shared cup, is forced to compare the power of spiritual water with the temporary life-giving power of literal water.

The sculpture also creates a sense of ambiguity, forcing us to ask who is giving water, and therefore life, to whom. At the same time it is clear that for the woman, a new life, bound up with the life-giving power of the messiah, has sprung forth.

The making of the Woman At The Well sculpture

A skeleton of steel rods, bent and welded, form a rigid structure on to which the modelling in plaster begins. Then the artist shapes the plaster with files and chisels.

When the model is formed, it is supported with chains and straps, cut into sections, and

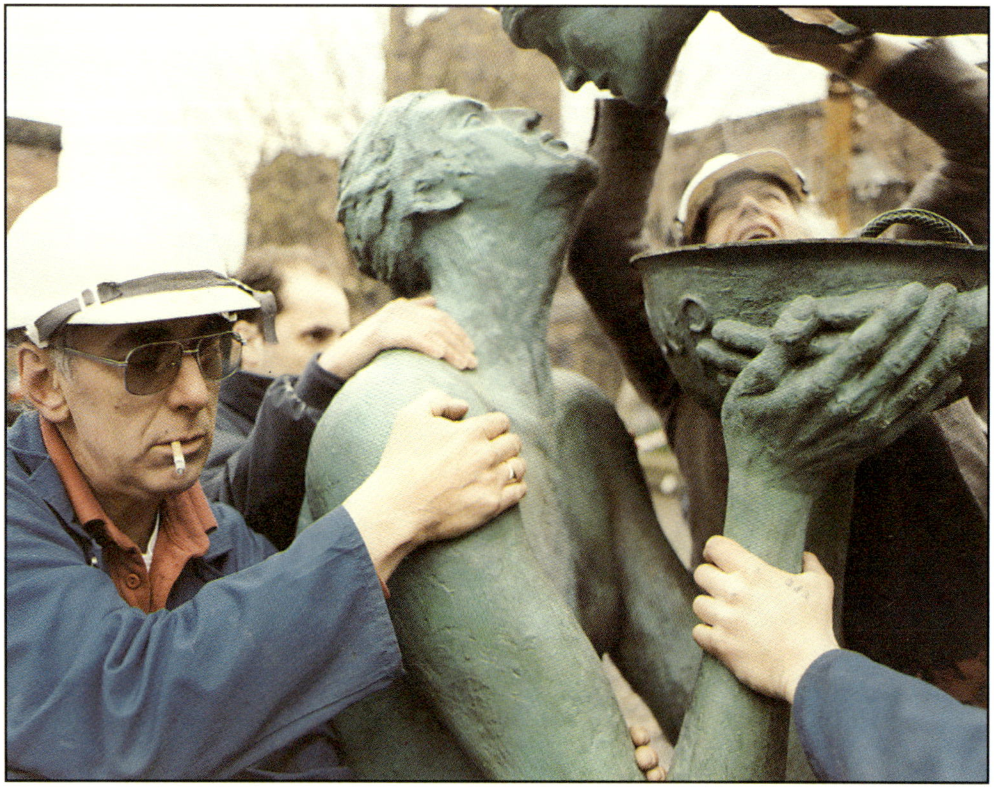

transported to the foundry for the casting process.

From the various sections of the sculpture rubber moulds are made, and into these hot wax is poured.

When this solidifies, each section is encased in a type of plaster. The wax is then melted and molten bronze poured in its place. The bronze sections are then welded back together to form the finished piece. Once complete, the artist applies heat and acid to achieve the desired patina. It is then sealed with wax.

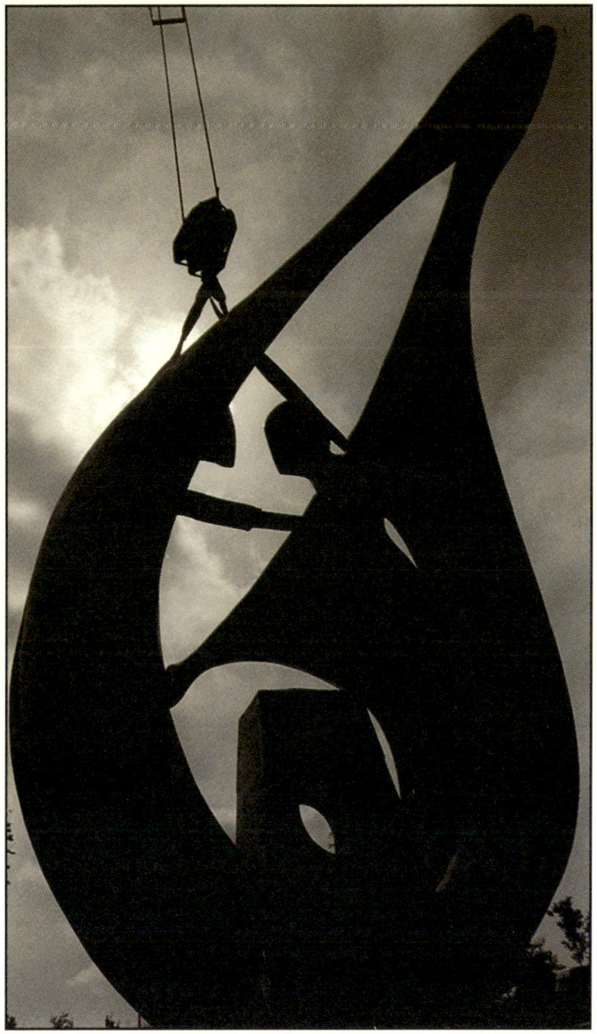

1993

CHALLENGE

This bold, powerful statement about individual achievement within a corporate environment was commissioned by CAPITAL BANK and unveiled in 1993. The sculpture, which stands outside Capital House in Chester, echoes the Bank's business ethos, and was specially tailored for a corporate environment.

"We sometimes speak of 'an inspired age', or a 'creative epoch', but then we are only speaking metaphorically. But the facts correspond to the figure of speech: eras, no less than artists, have their afflatus, and a society can be inspired. And that is the problem we should study - the relations between the forms of society and the forms of art, the interflow of vitality from organisations to individuals, and the generation of creative activity in the group, between persons and associations."
HERBERT READ IN THE PHILOSOPHY OF MODERN ART

The imposing 15 foot bronze sculpture attempts to express the challenge facing all individuals in a changing environment, and how they will measure up. In this sense it portrays a moment of self-revelation. The large figure confronts itself as though looking in a mirror, with outstretched arms striving to find some degree of personal measurement. Apertures in the sculpture give the piece a strong spatial feel, and a metronome feature provides a pivotal balancing element suggestive of time and measurement.

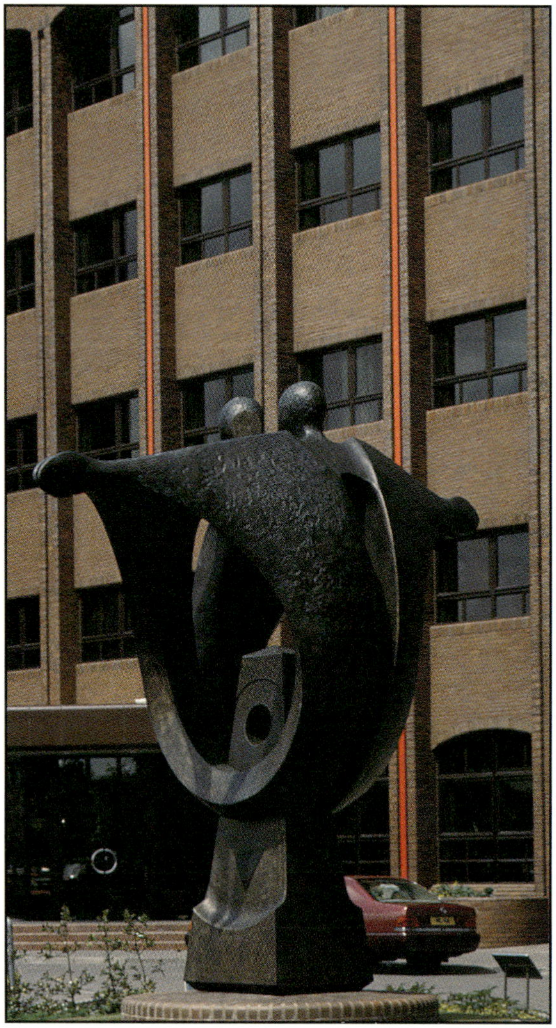

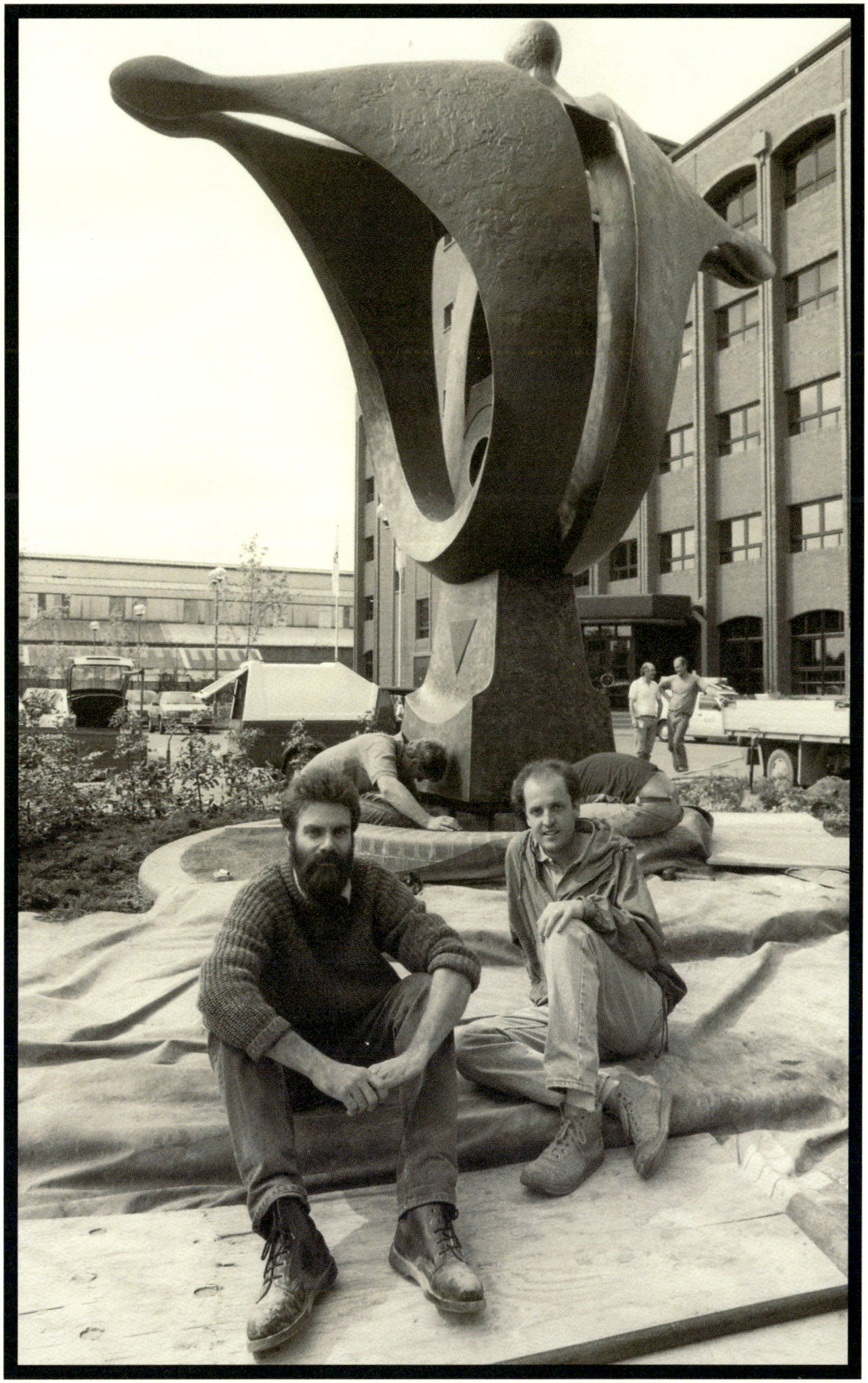

Rungwe Kingdon of Pangolin Art foundry assists Stephen Broadbent with the installation of 'Challenge'

1992

A Celebration of Chester

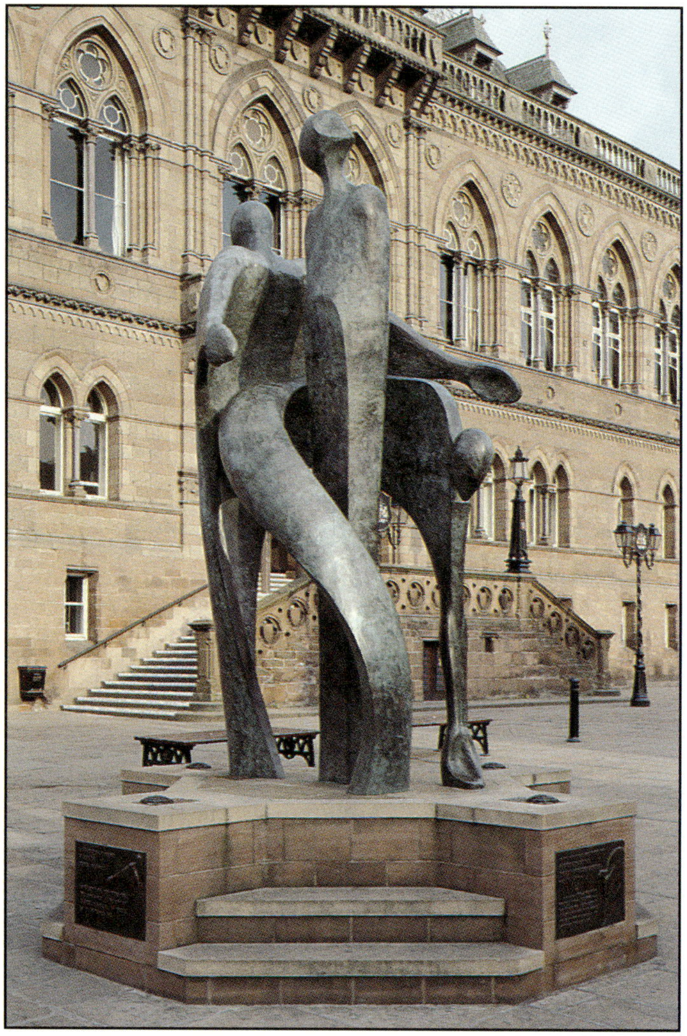

The 'Celebration of Chester' sculpture was unveiled in Chester Town Hall square in 1992 as part of the 900th anniversary celebrations of Chester Cathedral.

The project evolved through a partnership of civic, spiritual, and commercial interests that have sustained the city since its foundation.

These powerful institutions were represented by Chester Cathedral, Chester City Council, and CAPITAL BANK, a major employer in the area.

Giving shape to the soul of a city

The collective aim was to 'give shape' to the soul of the city, capturing the elements

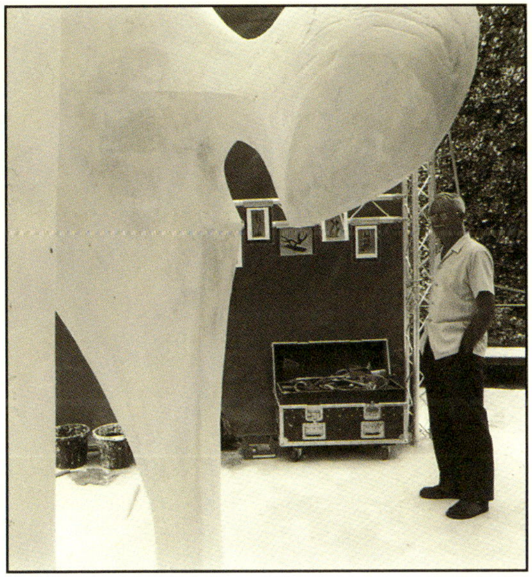

that bring health, prosperity and life to it. To effectively marry its religious heritage with its industrial wealth in a cohesive statement that would celebrate the continuing interdependence of Chester's collective spiritual, commercial and personal life.

The artist was awarded the commission in the summer of 1990. His brief, to create a sculpture that would appropriately celebrate the spiritual, civic and economic standing of the City.

As the first public sculpture to have been erected in the city for generations, its commissioning brought into sharp focus many of the issues that lie at the heart of Stephen Broadbent's approach to public art.

A public site is a far more difficult and challenging space to fill than that of an art gallery. Gallery visitors have time, and powers of discrimination on their side, while a passing audience have only the urgent tasks of the day to contemplate.

In the controlled environment of the gallery, where responses are conditioned by setting and motivation, the artist can indulge his personal vision.

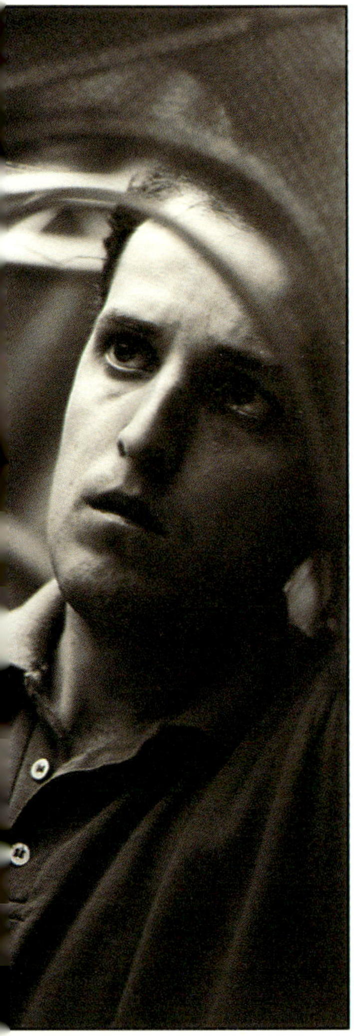

Participation the key

In a public space this approach would win not praise, but public disapproval. On occasion, the arrival of a work into a shared civic space is greeted with suspicion, disbelief, or even animosity by the onlooker. In this sense alone, 'Celebration of Chester' was one of the artist's most challenging commissions to date.

Broadbent realised that for the work to succeed he must find a way of translating his own vision that would strike a chord with the public, celebrate the dynamic of the city, and satisfy his own integrity as an artist.

The key to allaying fears and suspicions was to persuade the public to take ownership of the project themselves. This demanded qualities we do not normally associate with artists of the late twentieth century. Rather than working in isolation, to succeed, he needed public participation.

On the one hand this meant sharing and demystifying certain aspects of the creative process. On the other, it called for relentless creative control to prevent any dilution of the work artistically.

Finding the right location

There was another crucial factor to be considered. In a city like Chester identity is inextricably linked with history and tradition.

Here, the past can be perceived as familiar territory peopled by well-known artifacts, stripped of the energy and life that produced them.

The artist wanted to avoid this segregation of the past from the present creating instead a work that, although firmly anchored in the contemporary life of Chester, would look back to the past with appreciation, and forward to the future with hope.

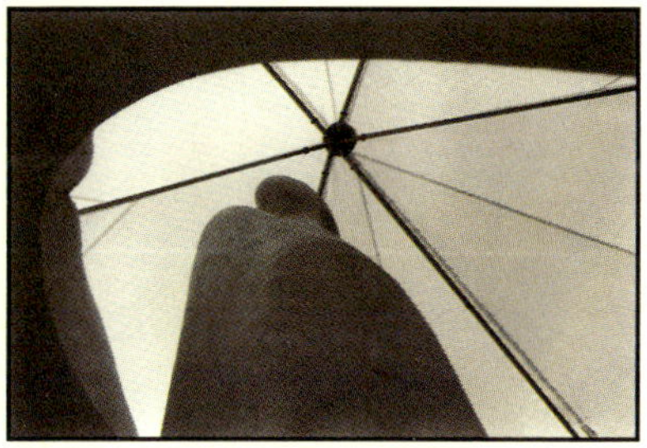

This meant developing a real understanding of the local environment, its architecture, its people and its personality, and finding a site that would do justice to the sculpture.

The choice of site was important because any public work has to relate to its surroundings. The angles, the light, the shape and style of nearby buildings all exert a strong influence on the eventual design.

When the Town Hall Square was agreed as the chosen site, Broadbent knew that its symmetry and towering buildings could present potentially disastrous problems of scale.

He did not wish to produce a dominating giant, yet for the sculpture to have impact, it would need to be of a sufficient size.

Careful judgement was required. After all, many a disappointed sculptor has fashioned a piece that is powerful in the studio, but lost in an outdoor setting.

As the symbolic civic centre of the city, the Town Hall Square was a daunting platform.

Yet undoubtedly this was the right setting for a work that would symbolise the achievements, aspirations, and strengths of a city and its citizens.

Two key questions lay at the heart of his research. On the one hand, what is a city? And what is involved in being a citizen? The Town Hall Square seemed to offer the perfect context for exploring these issues.

Celebration of Chester

Arriving at a useful critical 'reading' of the 'Celebration of Chester' sculpture involves taking into account factors that are external to the work itself. The most important of these is its location.

At one corner of the sculpture site stands the Town Hall, traditional seat of those elected to rule the city, oversee its welfare and organise its defence. Immediately to the north east lies the west front of the Cathedral, a symbol proclaiming 900 years of spiritual life, guidance and hope for the citizens of Chester.

To the south lie the busy shopping streets of the city, forming an appropriate symbol of the day-to-day working and trading routine that makes up a city's existence.

These fixed, physical locations hold the key to the form of the sculpture in so far as they symbolise in architecture the inter-relationship that exists between the city's spiritual, temporal and commercial life.

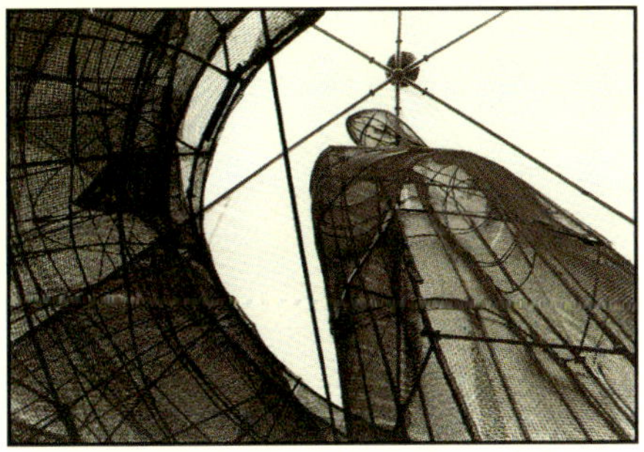

'A Celebration of Chester' carries these positive connotations further by expressing these relationships figuratively. The sculpture is made up of three large figurative shapes, not specifically of either sex or from any period.

The first, 'Protection' evokes the enfolding city walls and the security they have provided throughout Chester's history. Appropriately, this figure faces the Town Hall, the modern provider of protection and reassurance for today's inhabitants.

The second figure held within this protective cover is 'Industry'. Its spiralling form bends towards the ground, suggesting the work and effort every citizen expends to add to the health and wealth of the city. The figure inclines towards the shopping area, which is the centre of Chester's busy economic life.

'Thanksgiving', the third figure is centrally positioned, effectively protected by the other two figures. It looks towards the Cathedral, and in so doing symbolises the spiritual life of the individual and of the group. All three figures can be seen as individuals who are nevertheless interdependent.

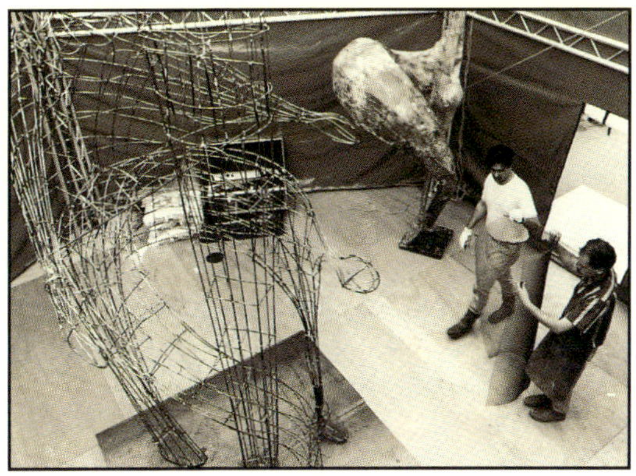

An imaginative solution to the problem of 'public ownership' was found in the shape of the 'Sculpture in the Making' project. This four week event took place in Grosvenor Park during the summer of 1991, and it brought the artistic process right into the public domain. In the beautiful surroundings of the park, Broadbent modelled the full scale sculpture, surrounded by countless helpers, onlookers, and passers-by. Before being cast, 'A Celebration of Chester' was first modelled in plaster, so visitors to the specially erected studio-tent not only witnessed the process at close quarters, but in many cases enjoyed 'hands on' experience.

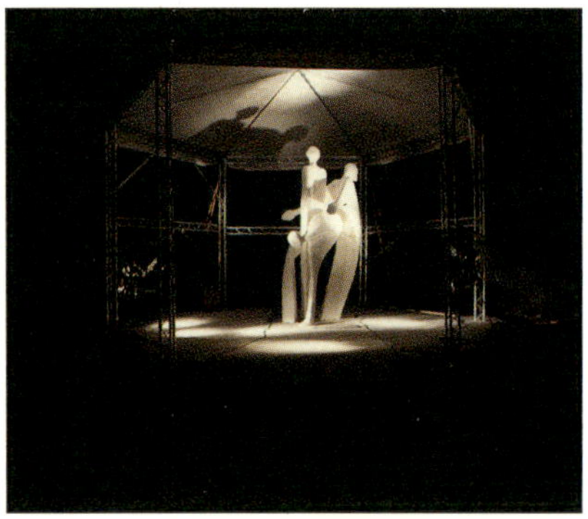

Everyone from students and schoolchildren, to grandmothers, welders, plasterers and office workers joined in, and in so doing struck a welcome blow against public mistrust of art and artists.

The making of 'A Celebration of Chester' in bronze

The initial lightweight structure, a skeleton of mild steel rods, welded together to form the basic shape, was built beforehand in the studio.

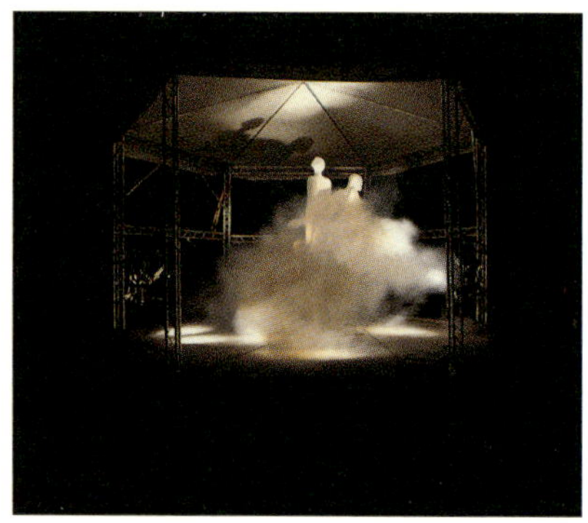

This was transported to Grosvenor Park in Chester, where work with the local community began in the specially erected tent.

The model was built up in layers, with a wire mesh placed over the mild steel skeleton. Then a layer of fibre-glass was added to create rigidity, and afterwards a coating of scrim or sacking was applied to help the plaster to adhere. After this, the plaster was applied, and when Stephen and his team were satisfied with the quality of finished product the model was transported to the Gloucester foundry to be cast in bronze.

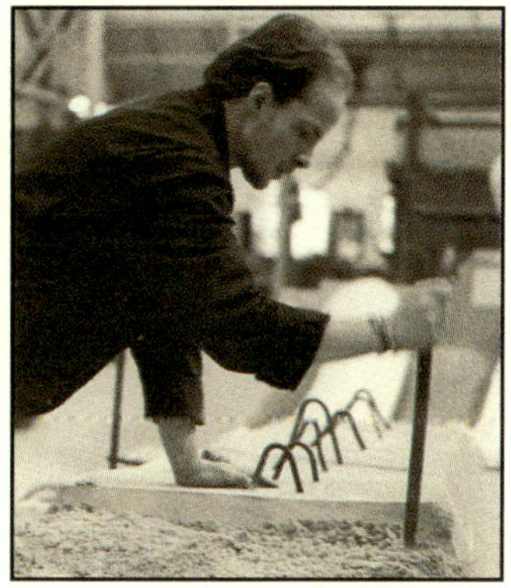

The first stage in the casting process involved enclosing each part of the plaster model in a two-part cast iron box filled with sand, impressing its image into the soft surrounding surface.

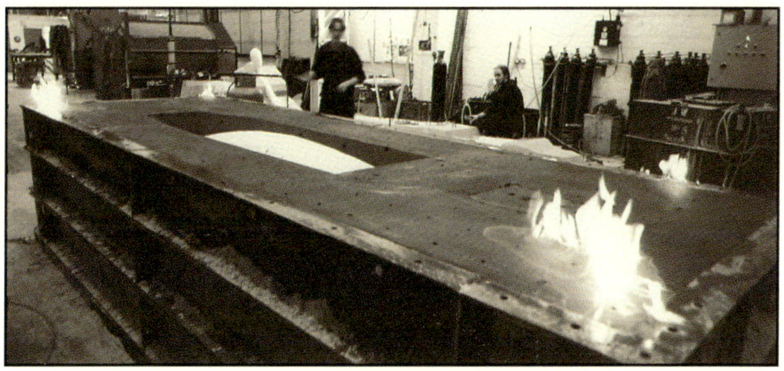

Next, the foundry craftsmen injected the box with carbon dioxide to solidify the sand. So, when the sections of the box were separated and the plaster model removed, they were left with two halves of a finely-detailed mould of rigid sand.

An outer mould alone would be much too heavy for the 15 foot high sculpture, however. A hollow casting was required, and this involved an additional and far more complex operation.

The craftsmen set about creating an extra inner and outer mould for each section. Then an inner core of sand was made that followed the contours of the exterior shape minus a quarter of an inch all round.

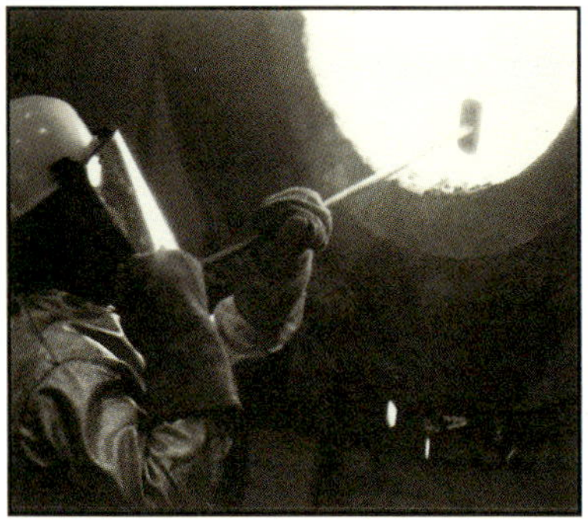

This was achieved by running a quarter inch-deep coating of polystyrene over the inside of the first mould, and then pouring in fresh sand.

Another injection of carbon dioxide followed, then securing pins were put in place, and the polystyrene removed. This left an ingenious outer and inner case separated by a mere quarter of an inch.

Next, molten bronze was poured into the channel. When this hardened, the sand moulds were removed, leaving a hollow quarter-inch thick bronze section which, after meticulous finishing, was welded to all the other sections that made up the sculpture.

1991

THE TRADES AND PROFESSIONS OF EDINBURGH

This imaginative project came about when Michael Grimes, then Broadbent's agent, put him in

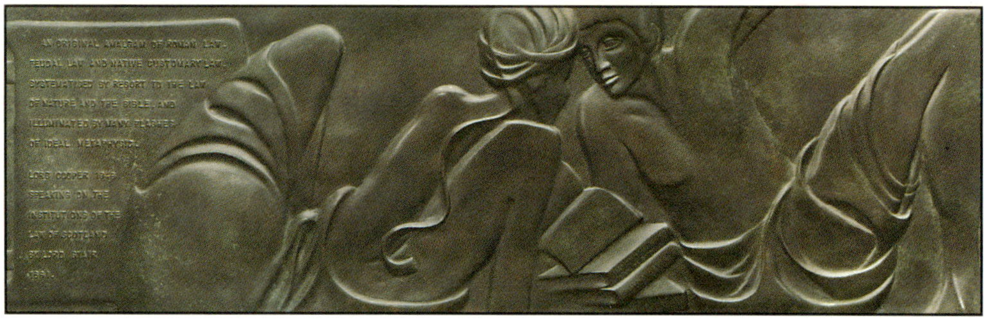

The Royal College of Physicians

touch with Gordon Milne, who at the time was managing director of the property developer Scottish Metropolitan.

Grimes played a major part in getting Broadbent's work back on track after the collapse of the art scene in the early 1980's. His strategy was to change the emphasis from exhibition work to commissions.

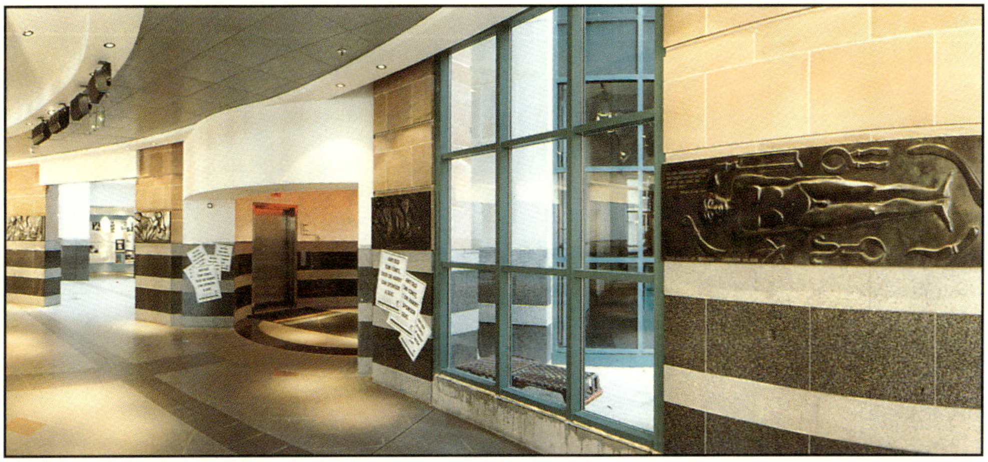

The drum foyer at Saltire Court

A series of nine low-relief bronze panels depicting the trades and professions of Edinburgh were commissioned. These would encircle the drum foyer of Saltire Court, a large new development situated on Castle Terrace, Edinburgh. This remarkable building featured offices, shops, and home to the Traverse theatre - famous for its contemporary productions.

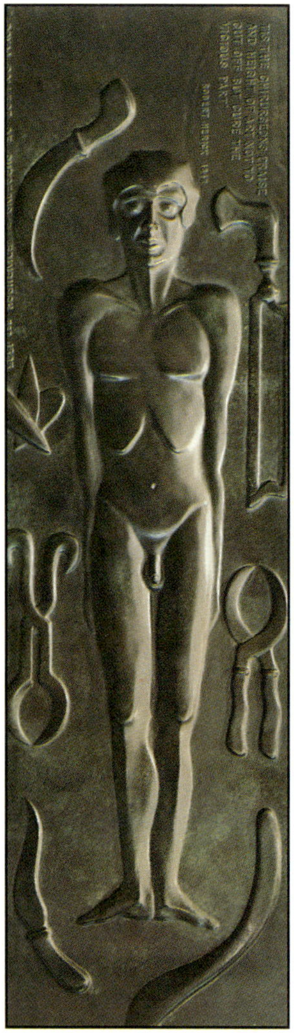

The Royal College of Surgeons

The intricate curved panels beautifully illustrate the impact the city's trades and professions have had on its development and history. Research for the project took Broadbent deep into the archives of the city's institutions, including Edinburgh University, trade associations and the Royal College of Surgeons & Physicians.

An ironic twist

With its innovative architecture, Saltire Court was an appropriate symbol of the confidence and buoyancy of the eighties. The elaborate bronze panels added to the effect, celebrating the history and achievements of a city that could look forward to a positive future, delivered by its own skills and strengths.

Ironically however, the precise timing of the development was to turn it from an expression of optimism to a poignant metaphor for the end of an era.

The first shadow to be cast over the project was the departure of Gordon Milne. He left Scottish Metropolitan following heavy losses incurred through the rapid decline in property values that hit the market at the beginning of the nineties.

Although work continued on the project, the installation of the panels was dismal and perfunctory. The fine bronze panels, intended as a celebration of resourcefulness and free enterprise suddenly became a reminder of its fragility.

Instead of attending an unveiling, Stephen simply fitted the panels without ceremony one grey Saturday morning under the curious gaze of caretakers and security staff. For Broadbent, this un-remarked and un-applauded event marked the symbolic end of the property boom and the beginning of a decade of uncertainty about the benefits of the free market economy.

1990

RECONCILIATION

Unveiled simultaneously in Belfast, Glasgow and Liverpool 19th September 1990

Harnessing the power of the image for good

From the vibrant and rebellious marks of the urban graffiti artist to the didacticism of Northern Ireland's political murals, the motifs of disaffection are now an unsettling feature of modern city life. In Belfast, large scale wall paintings can galvanise public opinion, affirming a community's ideas about itself, its history and identity.

The political equivalent to poster advertising, the images projected from these public sites impact

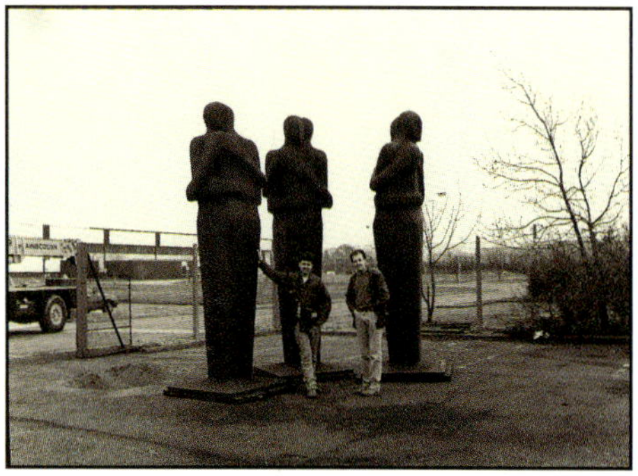

on people's daily lives, affirming a particularised view of the world.

In other, less politically volatile British cities, the intricate, often highly wrought designs of young graffiti artists are also powerful reminders that for many, creative energy is effectively dammed-up by society.

Yet still it finds a way to express itself. And, who is to say that, apart from its 'unauthorised' nature, artwork produced on the outside walls of a gallery is any less real than that which is hung on the inside?

Competing on equal terms

What if that power and energy could be harnessed and channelled away from confrontation and alienation towards harmony and co-operation? It was such thoughts that gave rise to the 'Reconciliation' project.

Broadbent saw that in Belfast, a towering figure that symbolised reconciliation could compete on equal terms with any large-scale paramilitary mural. Its message, the antithesis of images of struggle, conflict and entrenchment would at least be writ large on the landscape.

In Liverpool and Glasgow, such an installation could prompt a disaffected and disenfranchised youth to edge away from alienation in the sub-culture towards constructive participation in society.

In its two year history, the 'Reconciliation' project had a unique opportunity to test out these ideas first hand through the creation of three five ton, 12 foot high cast-iron statues to be unveiled simultaneously in Liverpool, Glasgow and Belfast.

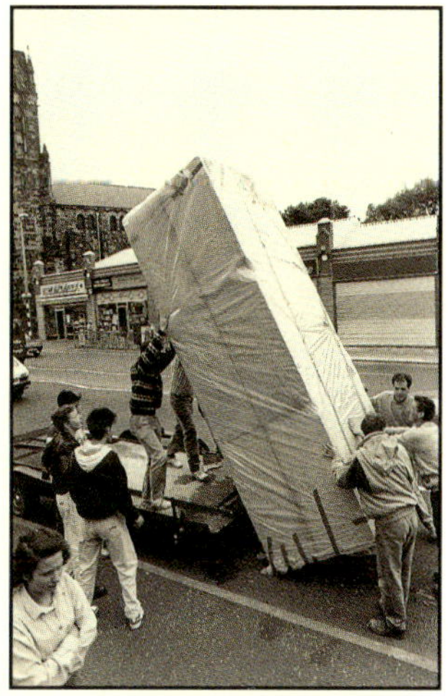

Although he works in various media, the vast proportion of Broadbent's work is figurative, exploring human relationships and struggles both in their public and private forms.

'Reconciliation' began as Broadbent's own very personal response to settling a painful difference with another person. Now, he had the opportunity to turn it into a metaphor for reconciliation between opposing groups embroiled in social and political turmoil in three cities with very different social and political problems.

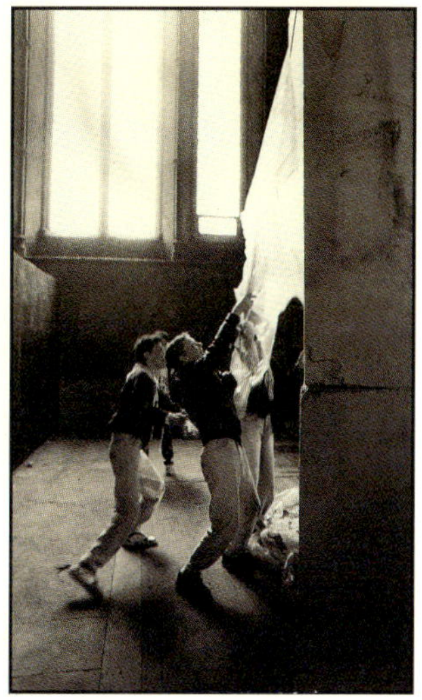

Through his sculpture the artist wanted to say something that was accessible, relevant and challenging. A work that could speak the language of unity and reconciliation to the three communities. From the moment the statues were unveiled their simple, yet powerful message has continued to be understood.

What is remarkable about the 'Reconciliation' project is that, unlike most public monuments formed by an individual artist away from the public gaze, it was created in partnership with young people from the communities themselves.

For Broadbent, this was a watershed experience. Working with people for whom the problems of social and religious disharmony are a daily reality convinced him beyond doubt of the genuine value and power of public art.

Broadbent freely acknowledges that it will take more than one sculpture to address and heal the heart-rending and seemingly intractable divisions in human society.

He sees the work not as a cure, but as a focal point for positive feelings. A tangible, positive statement about human nature that will remind future generations of our capacity to build as well as destroy.

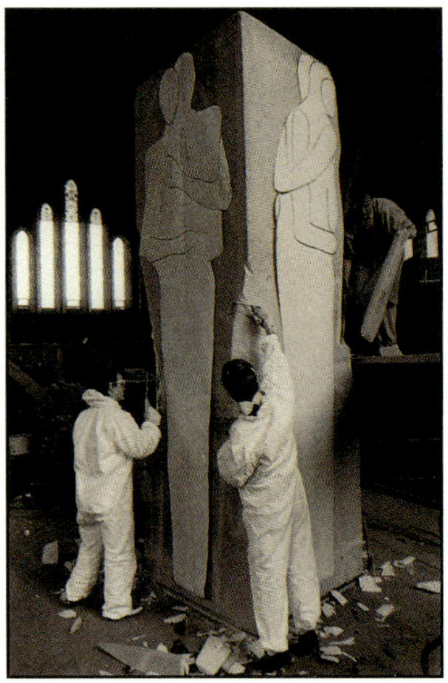

It is his hope that all people, of whatever persuasion will not only draw inspiration and strength from the statue but also work to realise the potential offered by reconciliation rather than dwelling on the mistakes and sufferings of the past.

Working together for 'Reconciliation'

'Reconciliation' was modelled in Belfast with the help of selected teenagers from representative localities of the city. Since participation was the key to success, each individual was made to feel part of the creative process.

The youngsters stayed with the project throughout, witnessing the casting and finishing of the statues in Liverpool, and being present at simultaneous

"The statue will be particularly relevant in Belfast, and the site chosen for its placing is admirably chosen for the purpose, since it stands on an interface between two communities frequently locked in conflict, but which have in fact much more in common than they are inclined or even allowed to believe."
CAHAL B. DALY
BISHOP OF DOWN & CONNOR

unveilings in each of their respective cities.

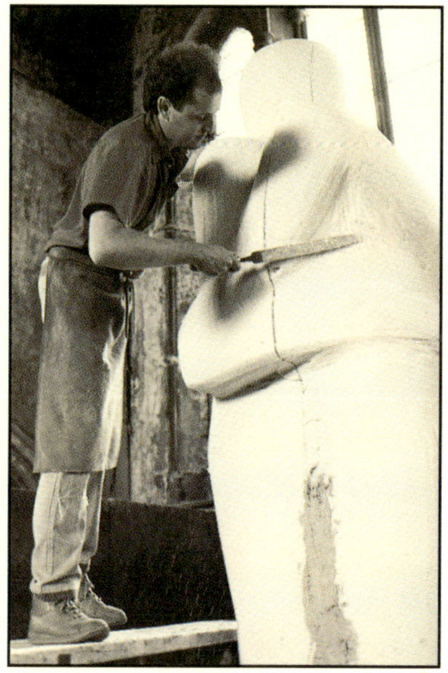

The team - Broadbent, his colleague Paul Greggs, Dave Williams, a professional photographer, and the seven teenagers arrived in Belfast to begin work on the statue in July 1989.

Their home for the week was a large house with dormitories and a communal kitchen and living room, belonging to the Columbannis Community of Reconciliation located on the Antrim Road.

The first task was to collect a large block of polyurethane from Belfast docks and deliver it to a temporary workshop in the Carlisle Memorial Centre located in Carlisle Circus near to the centre of Belfast.

The cavernous cathedral-like interior of this former Methodist church, situated near the proposed site of the statue, provided a dramatic backdrop for the first stages of the sculpture.

The youngsters worked together, combining research into the styles of lettering to be used for the wording with supervised work on the carving itself.

Meanwhile Dave Williams and his young assistant set about creating a documentary record of the project and the local community.

The emerging form of the statue was shown to visitors and the press at a specially convened open

'Reconciliation' was made possible through the loyal support of voluntary organisations, local City Councils, senior churchmen and local action groups. The leading bodies were: in Glasgow and Liverpool, the Council For Voluntary Service, and in Belfast, 'Bryson House'. Youngsters from the three communities who assisted with the project were: Emily Cromby and Zapher Iqbal, from Shorefields Comprehensive School in Liverpool, James Paterson and Joseph Wilson of Bellamine School in Pollock, Glasgow; Marion and Karen Rock of St Gemma's in the Ardoyne, and Michelle Granville of Hazelwood Integrated College.

day resulting in positive media coverage in newspapers, and on TV and radio. The reports featured the views of the young people who expressed their desire for peace and reconciliation in their communities.

In the space of one short week the team achieved what it had set out to do, producing a powerful and impressive 12 foot image that could now be shipped back to Liverpool for finishing and casting.

For Broadbent, the working and playing with this diverse group was a revelation. Over the first week, a group of 15 and 16 year-olds' from three lively inner cities, each with its own culture and problems had come together united by a common purpose, to create a lasting monument to reconciliation.

From concept to casting

After two months spent finishing the sculpture at the Bridewell Studios in Liverpool, it was delivered to Varley's Iron Foundry in St Helens where, from one model, the long process of casting the three statues in iron began.

The casting took place over a period of time, but at each casting members of the team were present as the molten metal poured dramatically, giving shape to the ideas they had laboured to bring forth.

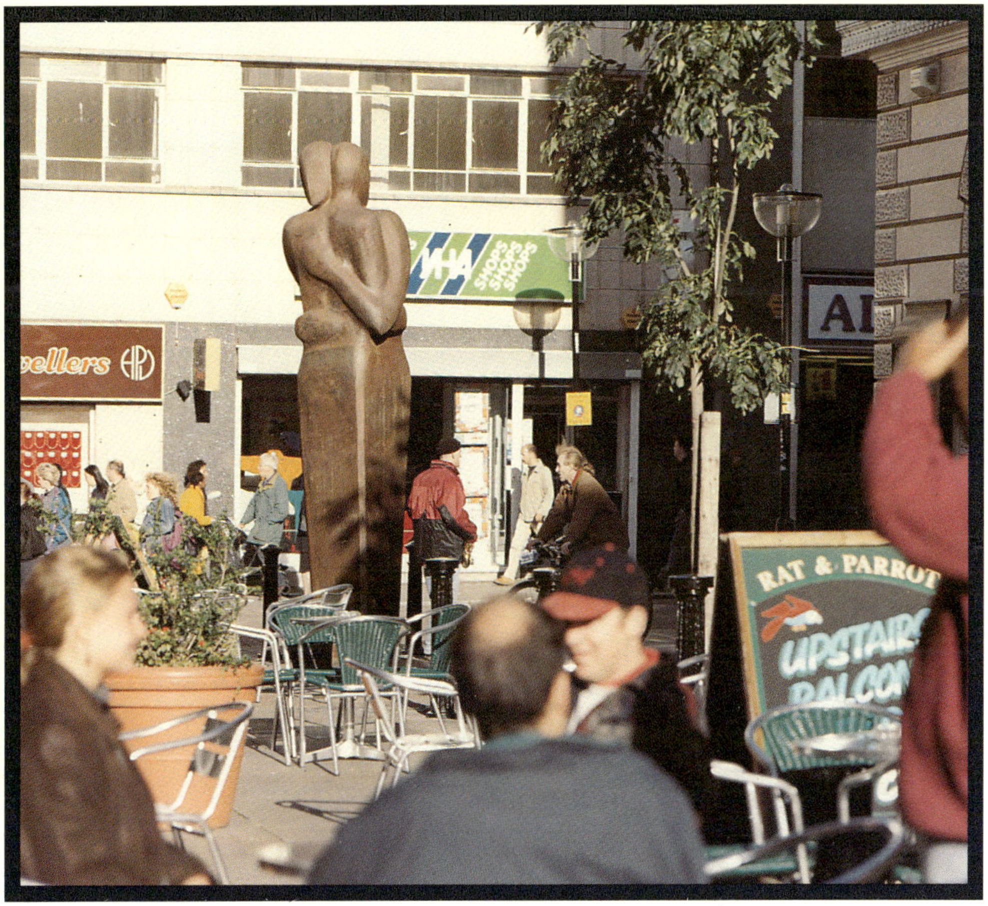

The sculpture employs the human form to convey a clear, simple statement about the desire and capacity for reconciliation in relationships.
It symbolises our need for oneness, with God and the human family.
The two universal figures become one through a timeless embrace. This unity is emphasised by the root solidarity of the form.
The individuals are effectively grounded in one another becoming potentially, 'one in body and spirit'.
The figures are universal, symbolically dissolving and transcending man-made boundaries of gender, colour and creed.

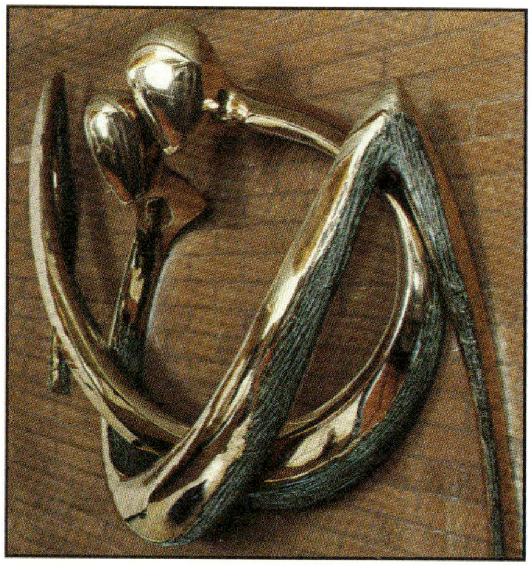

OTHER COMMISSIONS

1988

COMMUNICATION

'Communication' was a bronze commissioned for CAPITAL BANK by the then managing director, Harry Bush. It has special significance for Broadbent since not only was it the first large bronze the sculptor had completed, but it was also the first for CAPITAL BANK, marking the beginning of a long and productive relationship with the company, who have played a key role as a patron of the artist's work.

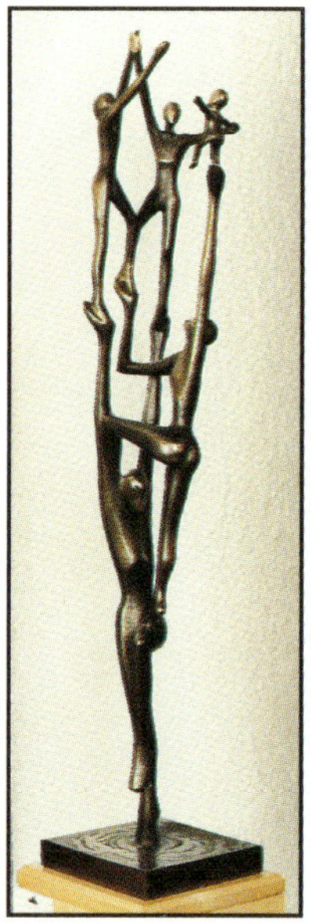

1988

FAMILY TREE

A 4 foot high bronze commissioned in 1988 by the Ethel Austin company and sited in the foyer of its head office in Knowsley, Merseyside. The sculpture employs the father figure as the foundation of the growing family tree. The concept reflects Ethel Austin's long-standing commitment to serving the needs of families through its business operations.

The owner of the company, Mr Ronald Austin, a well known art collector in his own right and the owner of the Hanover Gallery in Liverpool is another outstanding patron of Stephen Broadbent's work.

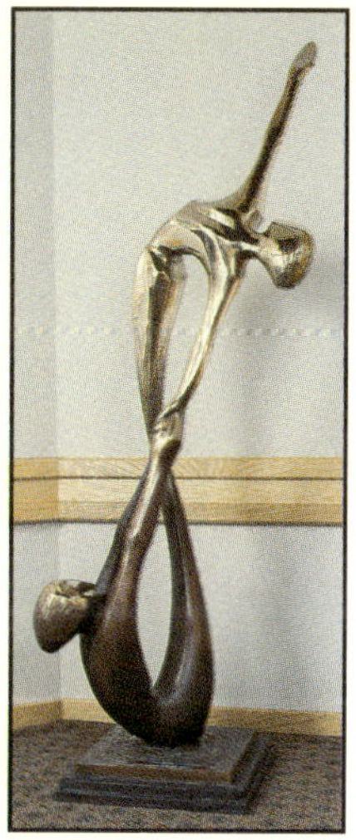

1990

A Time For Change

This 8 foot high sculpture was commissioned by CAPITAL BANK for the foyer of its head office in Chester. The sculpture, attempts to capture the creative tension that is a necessary pre-requisite of change. The rising figure strives for the new, supported by that which has gone before, suggesting constructive change within a context of continuity.

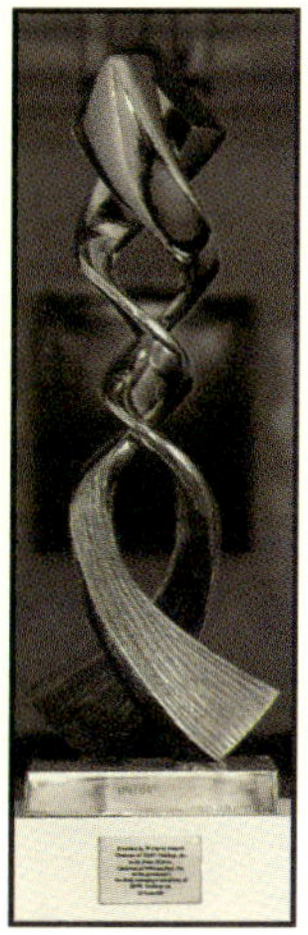

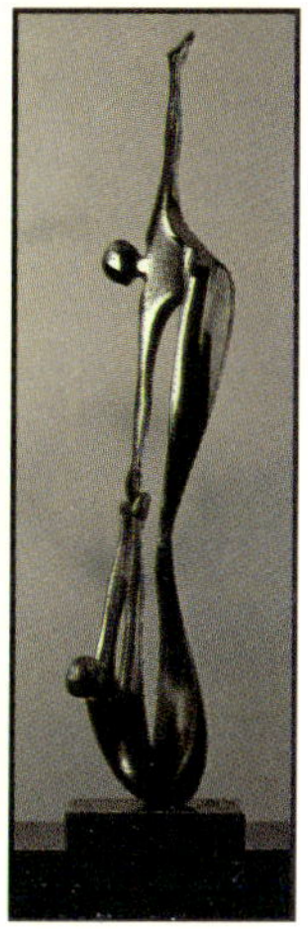

1992

Union and Common Goal

These two 3 foot high bronzes were commissioned in 1991 by William Purves, chairman of the Hong Kong Shanghai Bank following the company's acquisition of the Midland Bank. 'Common Goal', the original commission was intended as a symbol of co-operation and partnership between the two organisations.

In the event however, it was a second commission, 'Union' that was presented to the Midland bank on the completion of the merger in 1992, and is now on display at the London headquarters of Midland Bank. 'Common Goal' was purchased for the chairman's private collection.

1993

PROGRESS IS IMPOSSIBLE WITHOUT CHANGE

This 4 foot high sculpture was commissioned by Manweb for its Chester head office. At the time, the company was making the transition from a dedicated electricity supplier, to a more broadly based customer service utilities role.

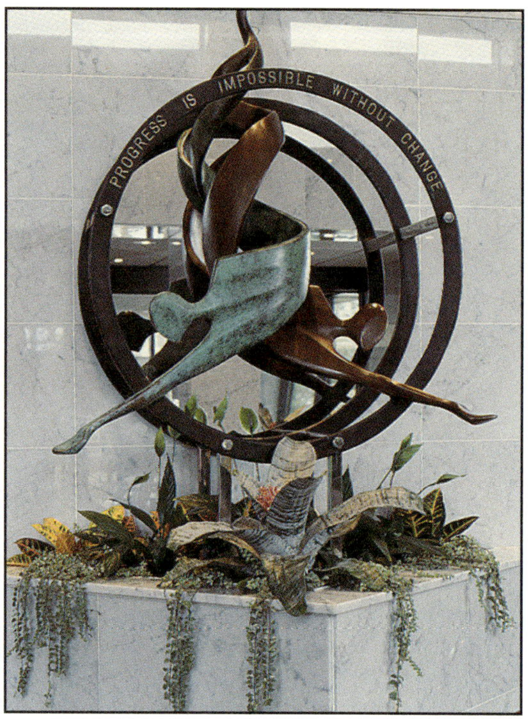

The sculpture reflects the company's hopes and aspirations during this period. The circle represents the earth, while the two figures represent positive and negative elements that, having evolved from the same root, reach out to explore new challenges.

Ironically, the sentiments of the work were tested to the limit following the acquisition of Manweb by Scottish Power which took place shortly afterwards.

Mersey Basin Campaign

The Business & Environment Achievement Awards Bronze

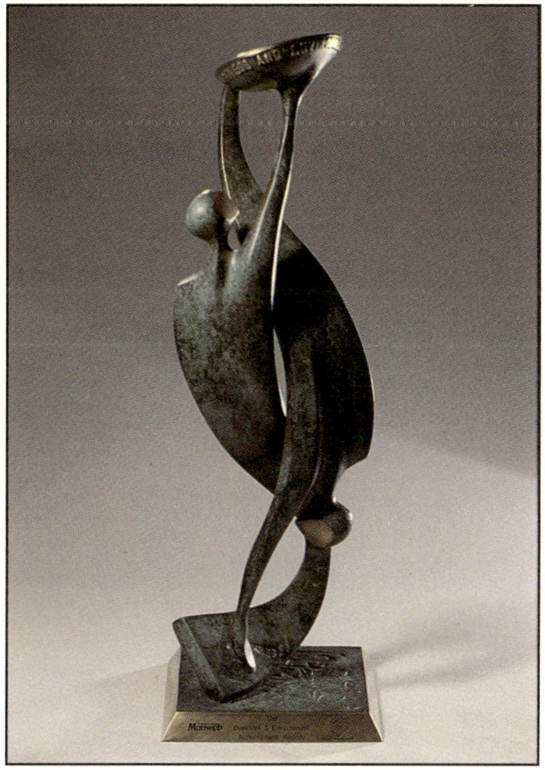

The two figures within this 20 inch bronze sculpture represent society. They take their form from the movement of water, and this symbolises our involvement with, and responsibility for this natural resource. Within the structure, one figure is supporting the basin which equates to the source of essential, life-sustaining water.

The other figure flows out from the basin, reaching down toward's the river's estuary, evoking an image of recycling and showing our need to put back what, in some ways, we have only been given on loan.

Work in Progress

At the present time Stephen Broadbent is working on ideas for a number of commissions. The following projects, all at various stages of the design and approval process show the depth and variety of his current work.

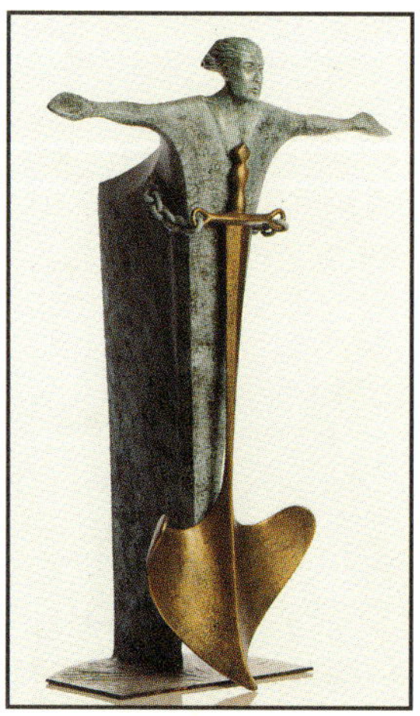

Christ Figure Sheffield Cathedral

One of Broadbent's current commissions undertaken for Sheffield Cathedral, is a public sculpture that celebrates the relationship between a Royal Navy Cruiser, The HMS Sheffield, and its adopted city.

The proposed site, with its central location within the re-developed Cathedral precinct demanded a bold and dramatic feature of significant scale.

When completed the design, in bronze and stainless steel, will stand approximately 15 foot high. The approaching viewer is greeted by a triumphant, welcoming resurrected Christ who is portrayed as though the figurehead on the bow of a ship. The outstretched arms complete the shape of an anchor.

The anchor/sword, manufactured in bronze is rich in symbolism. It is also a sword that becomes a ploughshare, a powerful reminder of the peace and the hope offered to mankind through Christ's sacrifice.

At the same time, there is recognition of the peace won through the sacrifice and bravery of the seamen of HMS Sheffield.

The plough, another great source of Christian imagery, can be seen as ploughing the oceans, a symbol that forges even stronger links between this land-locked city and the ships that bear its name.

Low-relief designs set on the flat sides of the figure give the viewer an opportunity to interact more closely with the sculpture. On one side, the designs will speak of the life of the City, on the other side, of the life of the Sea.

These designs will evolve, through consultation with the people of Sheffield as well as with the seamen of the H.M.S. Sheffield.

Pulling the Plug, Ringing the Change

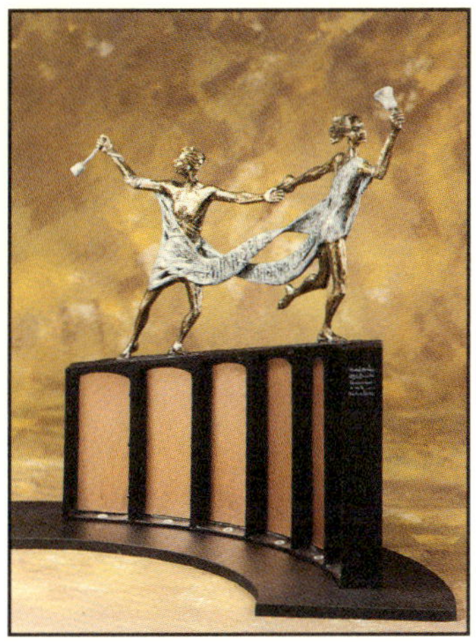

The Chartist agitation of 1838-48 was one of the most remarkable social upheavals ever known in the history of Britain.

The townspeople of Hyde played a particularly important role in 'ringing the changes' for social and political reform. Notable among these was John Bradley, a Clogger, of 8, Manchester Road who was responsible for helping frame the 'Declaration of Hyde Chartists' which demanded the proper recognition of the rights of the labouring classes.

THE SCULPTURE OF STEPHEN BROADBENT 1987 - 1997

On the 14th of August 1848 a band of Chartists, armed with guns, pistols, swords and pikes marched through Hyde at midnight, determined to effect a stoppage of the mills for a month by drawing the plugs of the boilers, thus bringing the machinery of the owners to a standstill.

These occurrences became known as the 'Plug Riots', giving rise to the common expression 'Pulling the Plug', which is still used today.

'Pulling the Plug, Ringing the Change' is a sculpture that recognises the important part the people of Hyde played in the reform of parliament, and their struggle to improve the working conditions of men, women and children. The sculpture has been designed to be sited on the corner of Clarendon Street in Hyde.

The design consists of images in bronze of two children running triumphantly, one holding aloft a 'plug', the other ringing a bell. A torn banner inscribed with the slogan 'Pulling the Plug, Ringing the Change' is draped between the figures creating a sense of movement.

A cast-iron base is used both to elevate the figures and to act as a symbol of a robust industrial object. This also accommodates the interpretative designs including the six point 'Declaration of the Chartists of Hyde'.

The copper panels that fit into the rebated cast-iron sections are of six contemporary children from Hyde. Each carries a significant object from the Chartist period including information on changes in the law on child labour that came about following the Chartist's activities.

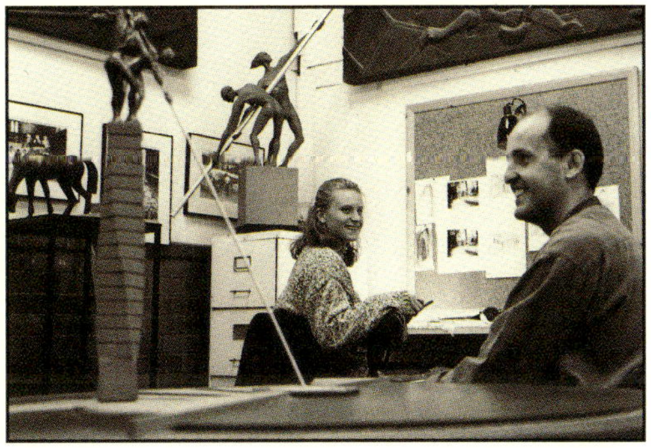

THE DARESBURY SUN DIAL

This ambitious project for the Millennium will, when completed be the biggest operational sun-dial ever made.

The proposed sun-dial is to be constructed in the shape of a circular water feature with a circumference of 150 feet, with 12 raised stone monoliths forming the face.

Broadbent was asked to create a sculpture that would add 'impact to this central feature. His response was to visualise a 50 foot central column divided into 21 blocks - one for each century, including the 21st. The blocks will be elaborately decorated with carvings of significant events from each century.

At the top of the column will stand two huge 18 foot high figures intersected at 45 degrees by a stainless steel and glass beacon soaring to 125 feet above ground level.

This landmark feature will not only mark the passage of time, but will also be a stunning focal point for the business park and its hotel entrance by day and night.

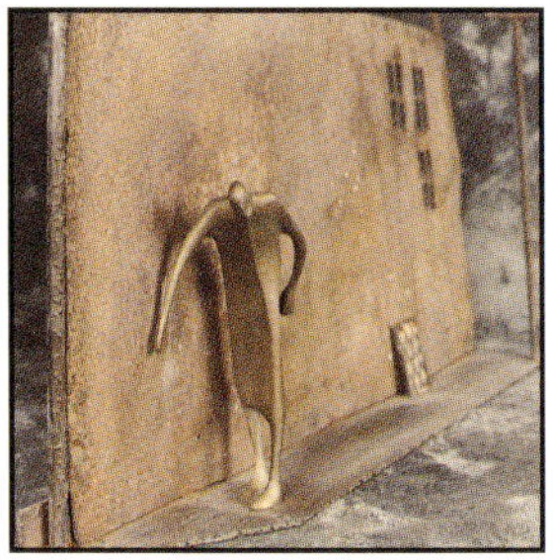

'Russia Sends First Woman into Space.' Bronze and steel

Any review of Stephen Broadbent's work will reveal a strong affinity with environmental, historic and religious themes. Although a Christian reading of Broadbent's work is the most obvious, the roots of his inspiration can be traced to two individuals who occupied completely different ends of the emotional, religious and artistic spectrum.

A love of tools and materials

The first was Mr Hickman, Broadbent's metalwork teacher at the Blue Coat school in Liverpool. "He was a silversmith by trade, and it was from him that I got my love of metals, of tools and of processes," he explains.

He discovered this passion for metalwork during adolescence, and claims that as well as giving him excellent practical skills and a sense of discipline, it also helped him form his sense of identity.

A passion for life

At school Broadbent won a place to study Three Dimensional Design at Sheffield. However, it was at this point that he met the well known sculptor Arthur Dooley.

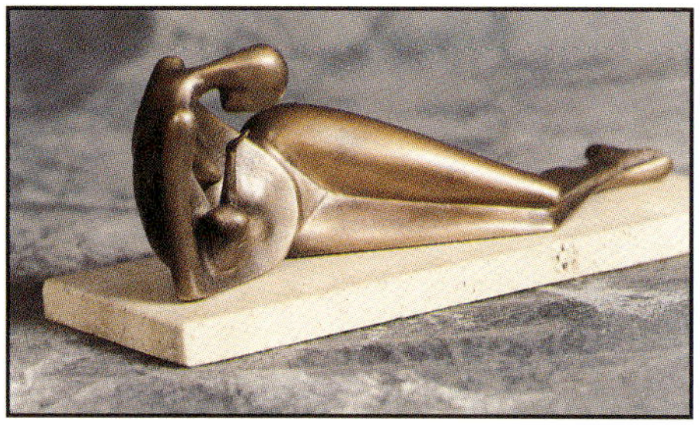

'Life' - a bronze maquette 1986

Broadbent was 17 years of age when he met Arthur. He got to know him through Dooley's son Paul, who was also a pupil at the Blue Coat.

In one piece of work, Stephen Broadbent accomplishes the rare feat of combining the imagery of the crucifixion with that of the resurrection. All the pathos, suffering and pain of Calvary is here but so, too is the energy and expectation of new life. The sign post leading to Liverpool held especial appeal for me, only surpassed by Arthur Dooley's addiction to the Madonna at the foot of the cross. In his inimitable and characteristic way he saw Stephen's work and unilaterally decided to rectify his own disciple's omission. Stephen made 'Life' while I was challenging British laws which have led to 5 million abortions and to the annual destruction, in British laboratories, of 100,000 human embryos. Too often, the issues are presented as a confrontation between a woman and her child, between life and choice. Stephen's genius is to remind us that to be consistently pro-life, not just against abortion, we must celebrate and be on the side of both the woman and her child.
David Alton

He was invited to visit Arthur's studio in the old Bear Brand stocking factory in Woolton. It was an experience that was to change his life. On meeting Arthur he knew he had found his vocation and decided immediately to move into Arthur's studio, taking his dormitory bed with him.

There followed an intensive four year training, 18 months of which was spent in Dooley's studio. It was this collaboration that shaped Broadbent's perceptions of art. During this period, he worked, ate and slept at the studio, and to encourage the young apprentice, Dooley presented him with a kiln for his 18th birthday.

"During that period we both believed that art could change the world. That it could literally touch people and transform their lives" says Broadbent.

Although he was not formally a religious person, Arthur's genuine caring attitude towards people and his complete lack of interest in material possessions made me see the link between art and the Christian faith.

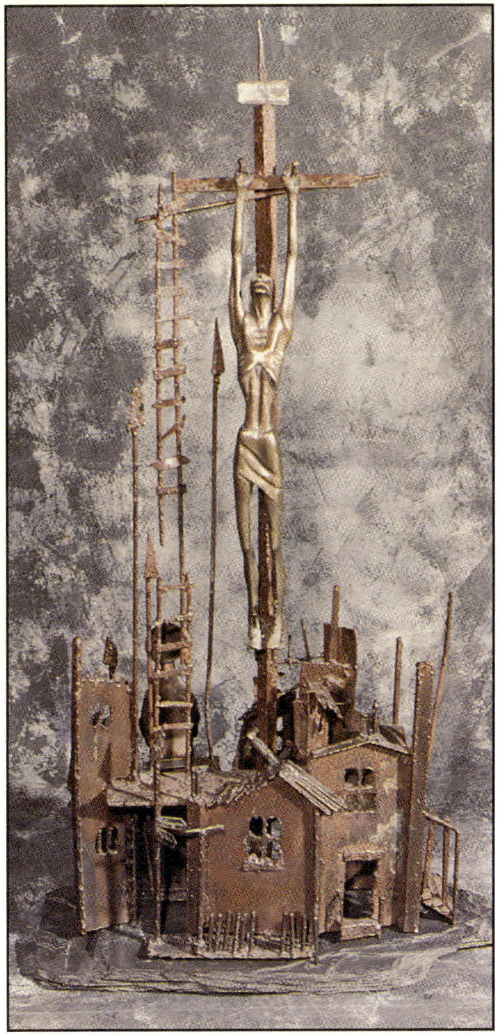

'Christ in the City' 1986. Steel and Bronze

Dooley and Hickman have remained as enduring influences on Broadbent's work. Hickman lit the spark of appreciation, imparting his love of tools and craft, and Dooley carried it forward creatively, imbuing him with a vision to which he still strives to remain true.

"Arthur Dooley was the most remarkable person I've ever met. He was a great ideas man, a great artist, and from the moment I met him, he was involving me in his work. He taught me how to think, and how to question." he explains.

A framework for creativity

Later, Broadbent was to embrace the Christian faith, and this was to be the final major influence on his work. His Christian world-view not only gives his art a meaning, but also provides a sense of continuity, accommodating his work into a long-standing tradition of art as praise.

"My becoming a Christian has obviously exerted a profound influence over my work. In the early stages of coming to terms with my decision, I even questioned whether it was right for me to continue in art. So in that sense it was a whole new beginning. When I decided to continue as a sculptor I saw it as a vocation, something I could work at with a sense of purpose and ambition," he concludes.

Rather than joining in the desperate clamour for the new, Broadbent prefers to celebrate history as a continuum of which his work is part. Although derived from a Christian world-view, he sees his art as a celebration of life, a key to unlock our understanding of the world we live in.

Broadbent's art is a door to the spiritual dimension. But it is a door that people and influences both from the secular and religious sphere have helped him to prise open on our behalf.

Arthur Dooley - Breaking the Mould

As with most characters who fit into the 'larger than life' category, no written words could ever contain or confine the personality and ideas of Arthur Dooley.

His obituary in the Guardian of Monday 17 January 1994 accurately described him as "the most colourful post-war British sculptor." This is true, yet Arthur was also a man who never reaped any material reward from his labours. In fact his generosity and complete disregard for money ensured he remained penniless for most of his life.

The BBC once made a film of his finest work, the Stations of the Cross, which he created for St Mary's Church, Leyland, near Preston. The film, entitled The Modern Passion, took first prize at the Monte Carlo Film Festival. Ironically Arthur, the 'star' of the show, received only £20 for his contribution.

Like a character from fiction

Arthur burst onto the art scene of the sixties like a character from fiction. A former heavyweight boxing champion of the Irish Guards, his loudness and intimidating six foot two frame invited comparisons with the roaring Dublin playwright and firebrand Brendan Behan.

Yet, like his lifestyle, his entry into sculpture was unplanned. After leaving school at 14 he had a brief spell as a deckhand on Mersey tugboats before joining the army as a boy soldier. During his nine years' service he was trained as a bagpiper and rose to the rank of sergeant.

His colourful exploits during this time sound like a Boys Own adventure. He served in Palestine and Egypt, then, on impulse stole a British tank, deserted, and went to fight for the pre -terrorist PLO as a mercenary.

His shipyard 'art school'

He was later caught and returned to the army, which put him in prison for a year where he whiled away the hours by modelling in sand and chipping at lumps of rock. Shortly afterwards he also converted to Roman Catholicism.

Yet even at this stage he had no plans to become a sculptor. That came later when working as a welder in the Cammell Laird shipyard. It was here, while helping to build the Ark Royal, that Arthur began to experiment in metal sculpture.

"The shipyard was really my art school," he told Peter Davies, author of Post War Artists on Merseyside. (1992), and he said he was "privileged never to have had an art education." In fact the closest he got to a formal training was sweeping up at St Martin's School of Art when he worked in London for a brief spell.

He also worked as a rubber moulder at Speke, where he developed some of his metal casting techniques. Though his acknowledged influences were Giacometti and Reg Butler, his highly distinctive style really evolved from his own experience as a manual worker in industry.

During his life Arthur worked in a variety of jumbled studios including a former Chinese laundry, a pub, and finally the former Bear Brand tights factory in Woolton - the only location big enough to house some of his work.

A master of paradox

Arthur's mastery of paradox was eloquently expressed through his simultaneous membership of the Roman Catholic Church and the Communist Party. While much of his work was political, industrial or religious, a great deal of it - including the Bulls which London Weekend Television commissioned annually as a trophy for the Cyril Bennett Award - was heavily formalised and figurative.

Arthur also had an eye for the ironic. In 1967, when asked to produce a multi-racial crucified Christ for the Methodist Church in Princess Road Liverpool, he responded by depicting him as a native American, later to become known as the 'Black Christ" in its Toxteth home.

His eccentricity and passion showed when he was chosen to do the excellent Fourteen Stations of the Cross in 1964 - a commission Henry Moore had turned down. In typical Arthur Dooley style he produced not 14, but 15 superb bronze pieces. His earnest argument that the extra station was needed to represent the victorious revolutionary Christ rising from the grave which was turned down by the Benediction was typical of his capacity for commitment.

One of Dooley's final commissions was the statue of St Mary, in the Mariner's Chapel of the Quay in Liverpool Parish Church of St Nicholas.

His work is also represented in the Walker Art Gallery and towards the end of his life he became Chairman of the Liverpool Academy, giving much encouragement to young sculptors.

No surrender!

Arthur remained angry about the London art establishment throughout his career, maintaining that art schools were doing no more than producing 'graphic designers for capitalism'.

In 1967 he even walked out of a London exhibition, which was being opened by Jennie Lee, the Minister of Arts, saying it was "too bloody amateurish." He personally resisted to the last, all attempts to get him to exhibit in London.

Arthur emerged at a time when modernism was exerting a real stranglehold on art, with an unspoken 'ban' on figurative work. Unlike his peers, and in spite of the fact that it was deeply unfashionable, he fought tooth and nail against this movement, producing art that went against the tide. Now, that tide is turning, and Arthur Dooley's example remains an inspiration to every artist who believes that even in today's commercially driven world, personal integrity still counts.

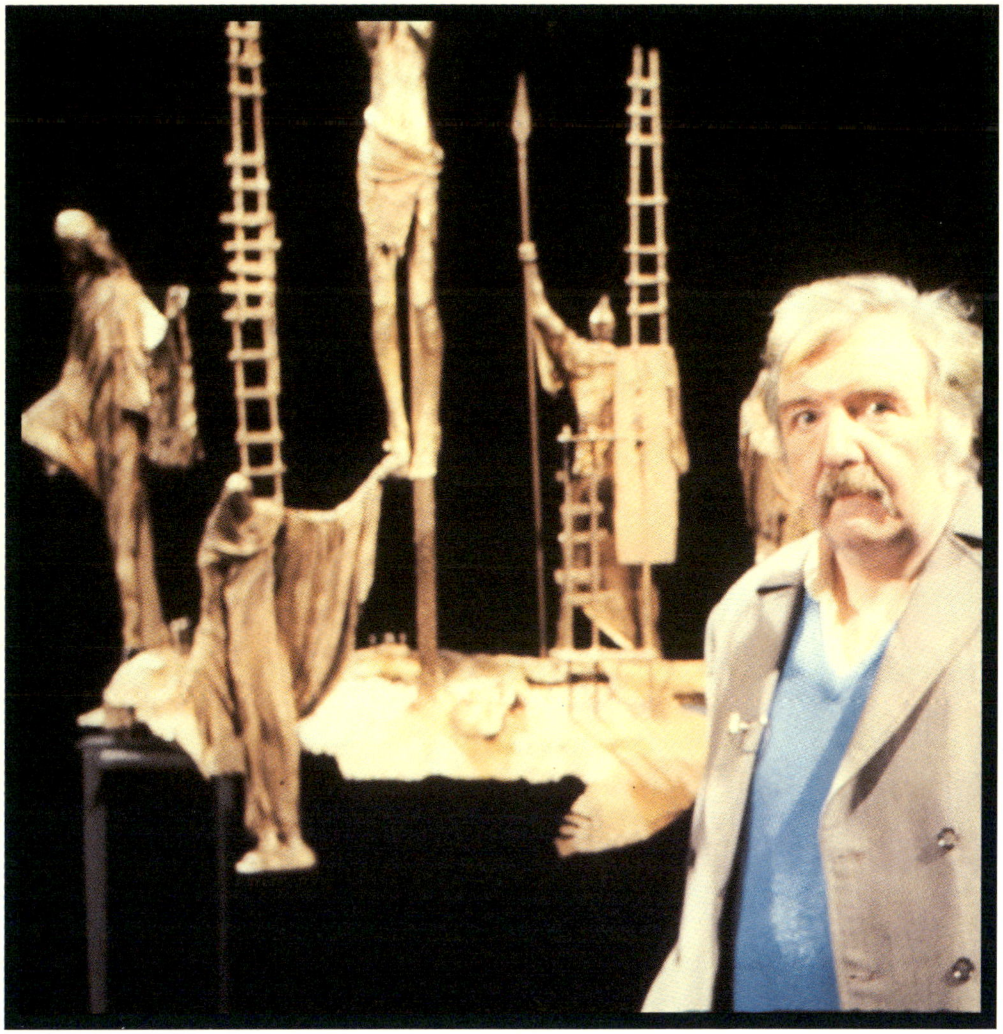

"Arthur Dooley's iconoclastic approach never endeared him to the art establishment, who regarded him as a maverick, and treated him as an outsider. As a result, the extent of his contribution to sculpture has never really been measured. In this brief appreciation I can never hope to put that right. But I can at least pay tribute to the part Arthur played in my development as an artist and as a person."
STEPHEN BROADBENT

The Role of the Public Artist - A Personal View

"Our present activities are futile. We take what exists - the detritus of a defunct civilisation - and we assume that by sifting it, cementing it, mixing it with bureaucratic gold or circulating it in unusual channels, we can re-create a past glory, build the foundations of a new civilisation. All we can create in that way is an ersatz culture..."
Herbert Read
The Philosophy of Modern Art Faber

In an increasingly agnostic age it is difficult to find in our cities a common set of values or aspirations that can be expressed through a civic sculpture.

Day by day our culture seems to become ever more fragmented and complex, and this is reflected in the contemporary art scene where artistic schisms not only alienate one art form from another, but also alienate the public.

In modern times the artist has been largely divorced from an established system of belief or meaning, effectively removing the framework within which the arts have traditionally been expressed.

The curse of introspection

The initial optimism of the first decades of this century, fuelled by the hope of modern science and technology soon gave way to pessimism. Sadly, with some notable exceptions, the artwork born of this period is largely a mirror for meaninglessness and despair.

By and large artists were encouraged to look ever inward, to reach the point where meaning and content within the work became obsolete. The result has been to prise form from content, alienating the viewer and instilling a mistrust of art and artists in general.

Modern artists who have followed the path of introspection have, it seems merely succeeded in exposing the negative aspects of our humanity.

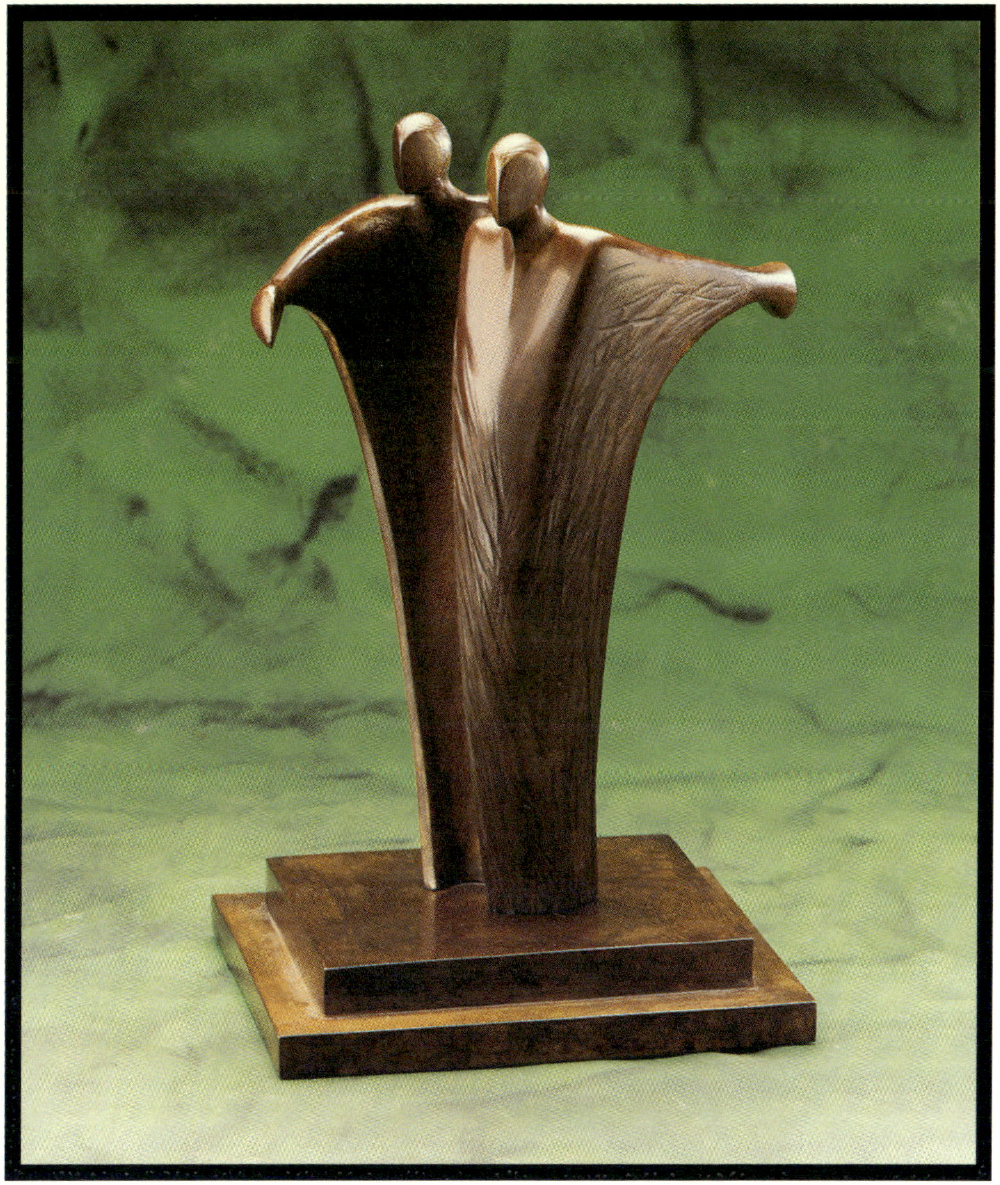

'Refuge'. Bronze maquette. 19 inch high. Limited edition of 8

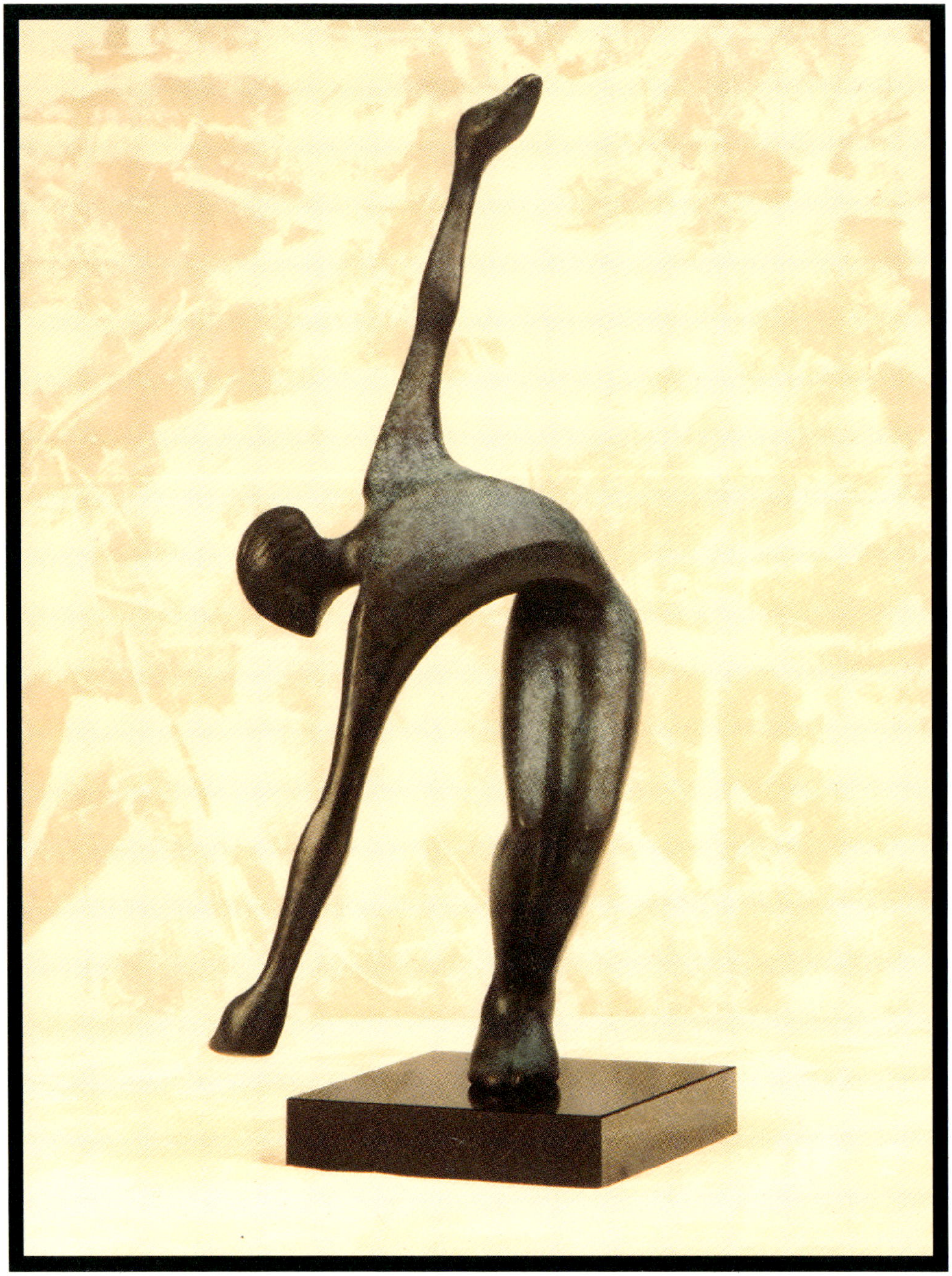

'With all your Strength'. Bronze maquette. 23 inch high. Limited edition of 8

This drive inwards has replaced the former social role occupied by the artist, a role that is affirmative, and that offers hope to our communities.

Thankfully, artists are now beginning to escape from this insular world and are renewing their confidence in art, both as a means of personal expression and, more significantly, as a means of enabling the public to understand and find meaning in works of art.

Redressing the balance

Historically, public statuary is portrayed through large bronzes of leading civic dignitaries who hopefully symbolise the ideals of their city. Some statues commemorate a significant national or civic event, while others affirm a religious belief.

Public awareness and appreciation of such works varies considerably. Some have lost their original meaning and now serve only to clutter up our city squares, yet others help create a real sense of place, providing a focus for civic pride, and a genuine feeling of community.

Creating an effective and permanent public art work is a serious responsibility. Where the contemporary sculptor has greater freedom for personal expression within the context of an art gallery or studio, the public artist does not.

In the private sphere the artist can experiment with new materials that may be completely unsuitable for a public site. He can be confrontational, presenting ideas that are serious, difficult or even transitory on the basis of personal interpretation. The public artist cannot afford this degree of self-indulgence.

Also, in a gallery setting, viewers can choose to accept or reject the work, stay or leave. Viewers of permanent, publicly sited work enjoy far less choice however, and may even express alarm when confronted with a large sculpture that arrives literally 'on their doorstep'.

In view of this an artist's personal interpretations are inevitably open to challenge where creating a permanent sculpture for a public space is involved.

The artist must show appropriate respect for the shared values of others in the community, as well as for the immediate environment, choosing his subject matter and materials with care.

It is right for people to feel proud and protective of their physical environment. We need to be secure about our origins and have some knowledge of our heritage. It is important to have a sense of belonging and identity, while avoiding the fallacy that we are witnessing an inevitable decline from some romantic 'golden age' - a mode of thinking that tragically, denies the real potential for good that exists within our own generation.

The way forward

I believe that the new patrons of art and architecture in the public and private sectors have a responsibility to take calculated risks with living artists and crafts people. To encourage collaboration on projects that will enhance and humanise our living and working environments.

History shows that art can be used for negative purposes - as in the case of state propaganda used by totalitarian regimes.

It follows that we need images and symbols in our cities that will promote life, new meaning and hope among people. An art that is capable of challenging the way we perceive reality, and that can, in some way transcend the mundane features of our lives.

All this involves an element of risk. Councillors are sensitive to adverse criticism, and directors are accountable to their board and shareholders. So it takes belief in the process, and people with vision to see it through.

I believe that the rewards can be great, not just for those directly involved, but for the wider public, whose eyes and minds are stimulated for good or for bad by the images that surround them."

Stephen Broadbent 1997

When, in years to come critics review the work of the sculptor Stephen Broadbent, how will his contribution to sculpture be evaluated?

A social messenger?

Some will define Broadbent as an artist who uses his work as a weapon for social change. That the street-level appeal of his public art, and his Christianity is, effectively part of a modern-day social gospel that preaches radical change through self-realisation.

In response, he would argue that his art is certainly a medium for communicating simple messages - often about human relationships - within a social setting. He would add that he is genuinely interested in changing things for the better. None of this, however singles him out as the preacher of a socio-religious gospel propagated through art.

No prescriptions

As an artist Broadbent believes in the simple capacity of humankind to reconcile, to make amends, to wonder and to discover. It is these qualities, rather than prescriptions or messages that hold the key to understanding his work.

As an artist Broadbent is more interested in encouraging participation than in preaching an explicitly social or religious gospel. Ultimately, he wants the work itself to be a silent, but powerful witness to the framework of beliefs and values that produced it.

Because his work often re-visits the most dramatic incidents and themes ever rehearsed on the stage of human experience, it can act as a catalyst, touching people's lives in a profound way, revealing truths outside their own experience, and leading them on to new realisations about themselves and others.

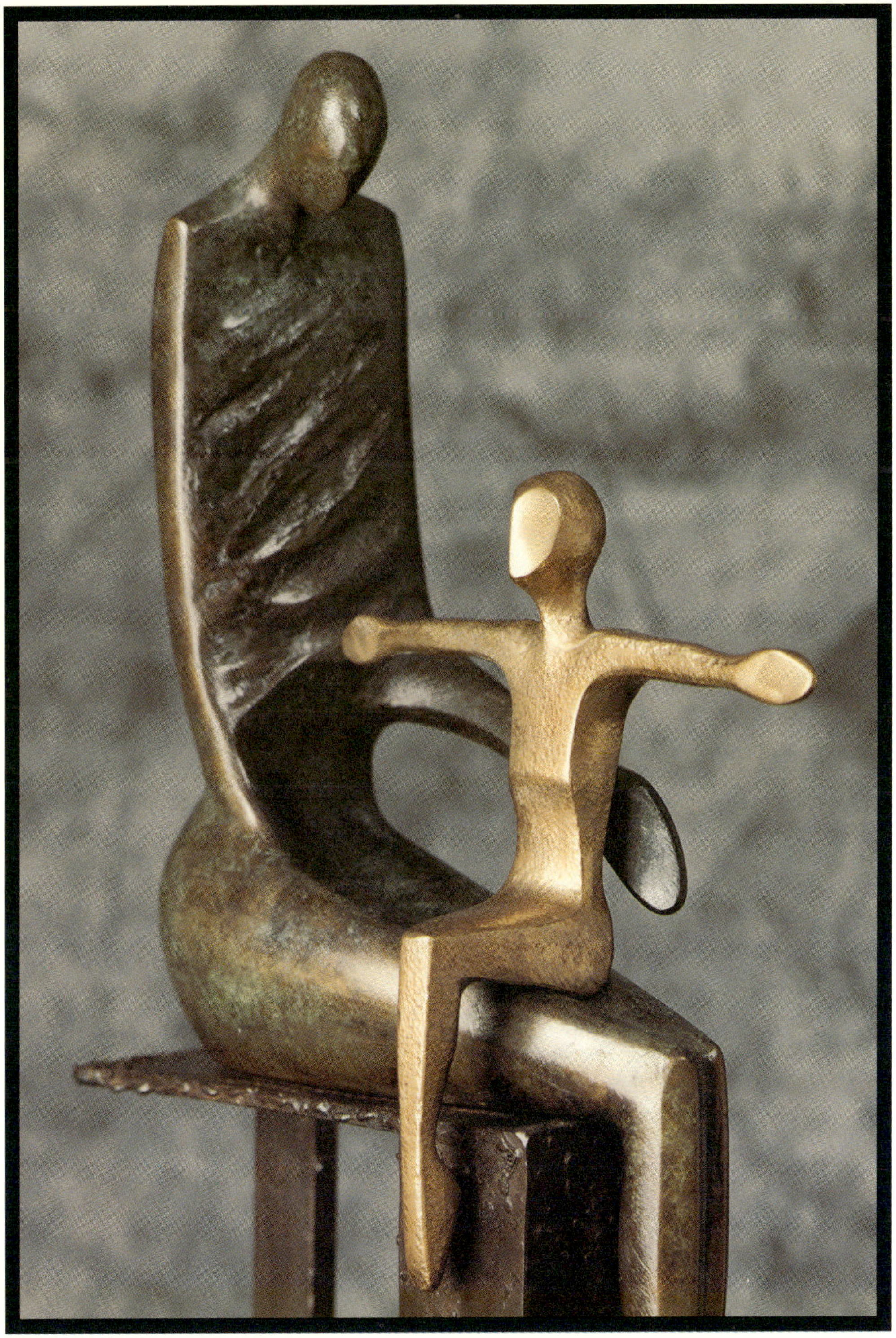

'Mothers Love'. Bronze/Steel maquette. 20 inch high. Limited edition of 8

A moral universe

However, although a fervent believer that art has the capacity to change people within a framework of Christian ethics, he refuses to allow his work to become a tool for didacticism, preferring instead to keep an open mind.

There remains a universal search for spirituality, but within a loose and accommodating framework. Beauty and truth, not instruction and dogma, are the keys with which we unlock our spiritual nature he maintains.

The idea that God is beauty and the belief that it is his creation that draws us to God, is what moves him to go on producing art that has the potential to motivate the believer and the non-believer alike.

The Oak farm project

Broadbent's long-term aim is to create an environment where self-discovery and art come together. It is hoped that a derelict farm in south Liverpool will be the realisation of this ambition. Oak Farm is envisaged as a residential centre.

Its function would be to provide an environment away from the everyday, where visitors have time to pause, think about and experiment with creative processes. The Farm would accommodate six to eight people at a time who would live and work together for a week or a weekend.

The groups would work closely with artist in residence in numerous fully equipped studios. At the end of each session an exhibition would be held of work produced.

Broadbent believes the availability of such a centre would fill a vital gap for aspiring artists, giving them the opportunity to develop their ideas, and the encouragement to succeed through supportive teaching and teamwork.

Public, Corporate and Ecclesiastical

For Broadbent, the Public, Corporate and Ecclesiastical areas are alive with opportunities. Expansion into these sectors will demand a considerably larger team, and he believes that by setting up the residential project he could nurture the right blend of talents for the job.

Our town and city centres, crying out for fresh design ideas, are a prime target for Broadbent's creativity.

Experience gained from re-designing Upper Bridge Street, Warrington following the IRA bomb, has

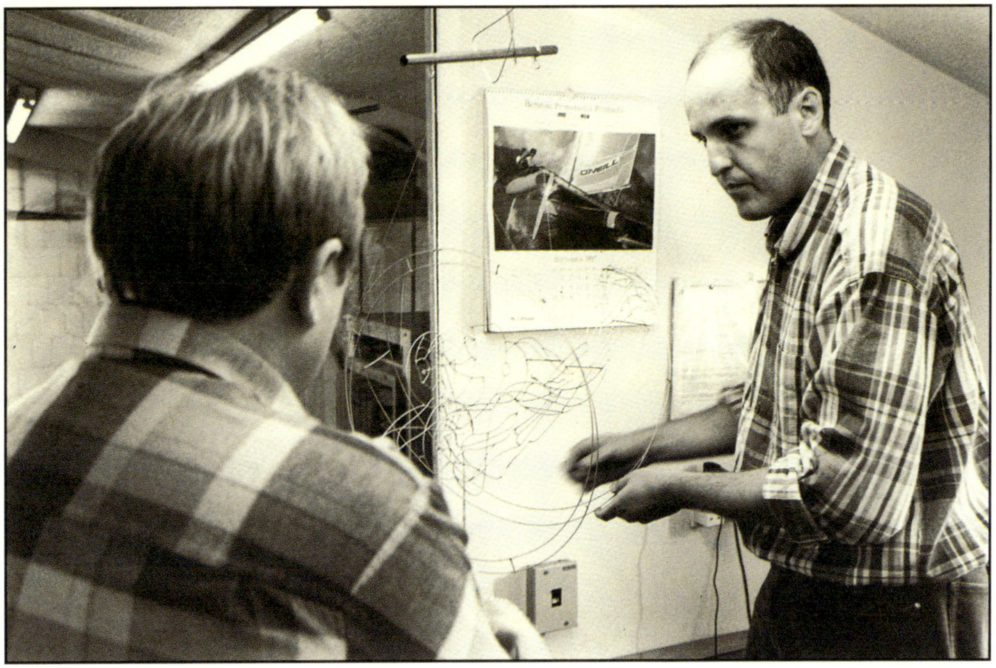

inspired a plan designed to bring life and vigour to the street-scapes of the UK's towns and cities.

This would mean employing architects and landscape designers with the skills and the vision to see his projects through on behalf of the public.

Ecclesiastical commissions

In the ecclesiastical sphere he intends to create a mobile exhibition of sculptures based upon the Gospel of John to take on a national tour of Britain's cathedrals.

As a member of the Fabric Committee of Chester Cathedral Broadbent is fascinated by design in an ecclesiastical setting, and has recently been involved in the re-ordering of the interior of St Cyprian's Church in Edge Lane, Liverpool.

In addition he would like to see his own private work for the Bruton Street Gallery developed further, allowing him to hone his creative skills for the benefit of the private as well as the public market.

Tinker, tailor, soldier, artist

In the final analysis Broadbent wants artists to be accepted as a valued part of human society.

To be reinstated as professionals, rather than banished to the margins, or lionised as progressive eccentrics by the establishment.

For this to happen, artists need to think positively, to be willing to co-operate and work as part of a team, to perceive their creativity as an essential life skill, rather than as a unique and mysterious gift that sets them apart from others. They also need to have the finances, tools and equipment to realise their ideas, and the vision to persuade others of their value. Armed with these things, a clear brief and a dash of courage, Stephen Broadbent believes that artists will yet achieve great things.

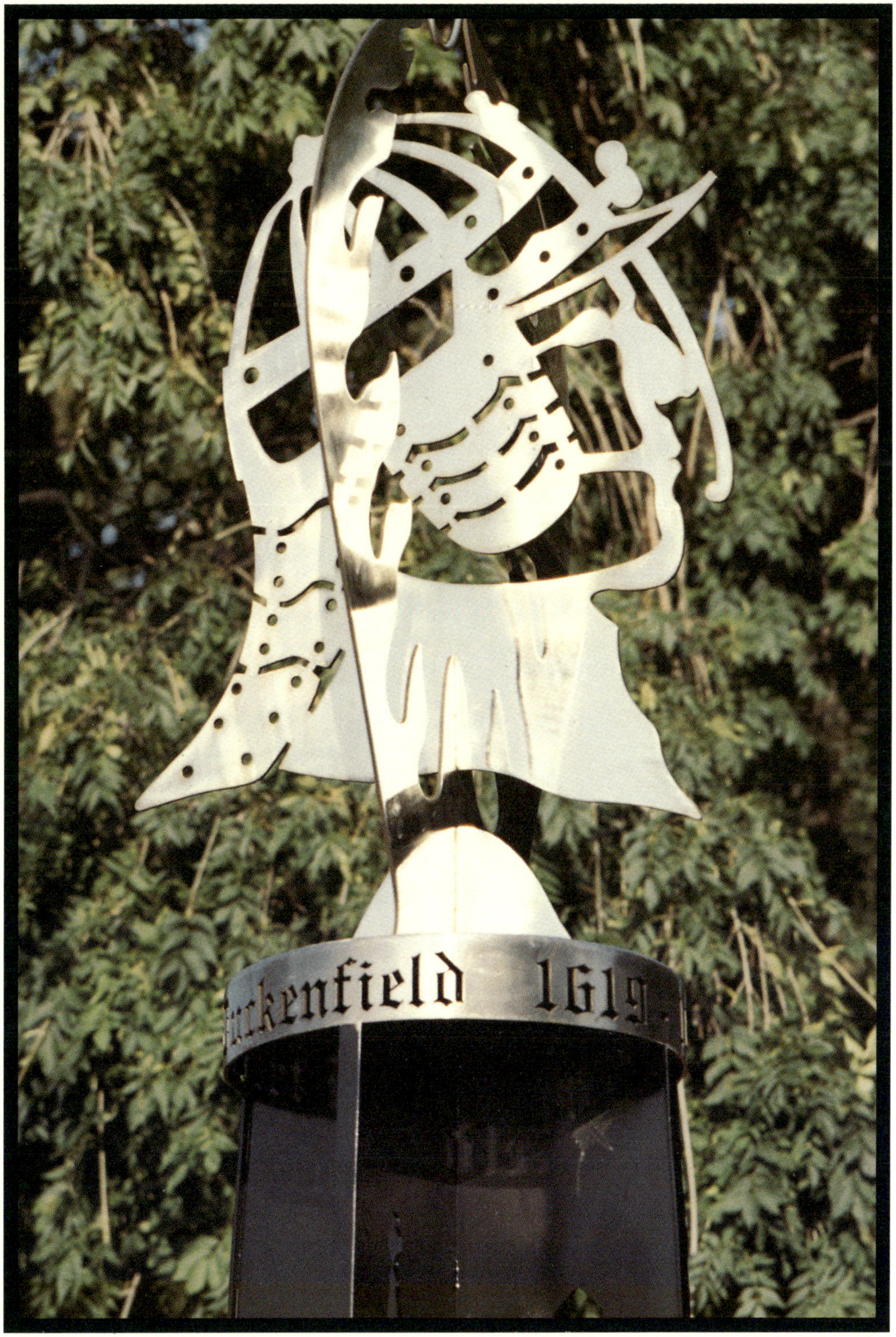

'Colonel Duckenfield'. Dukenfield Park, Thameside. Stainless Steel 12 foot high. 1996

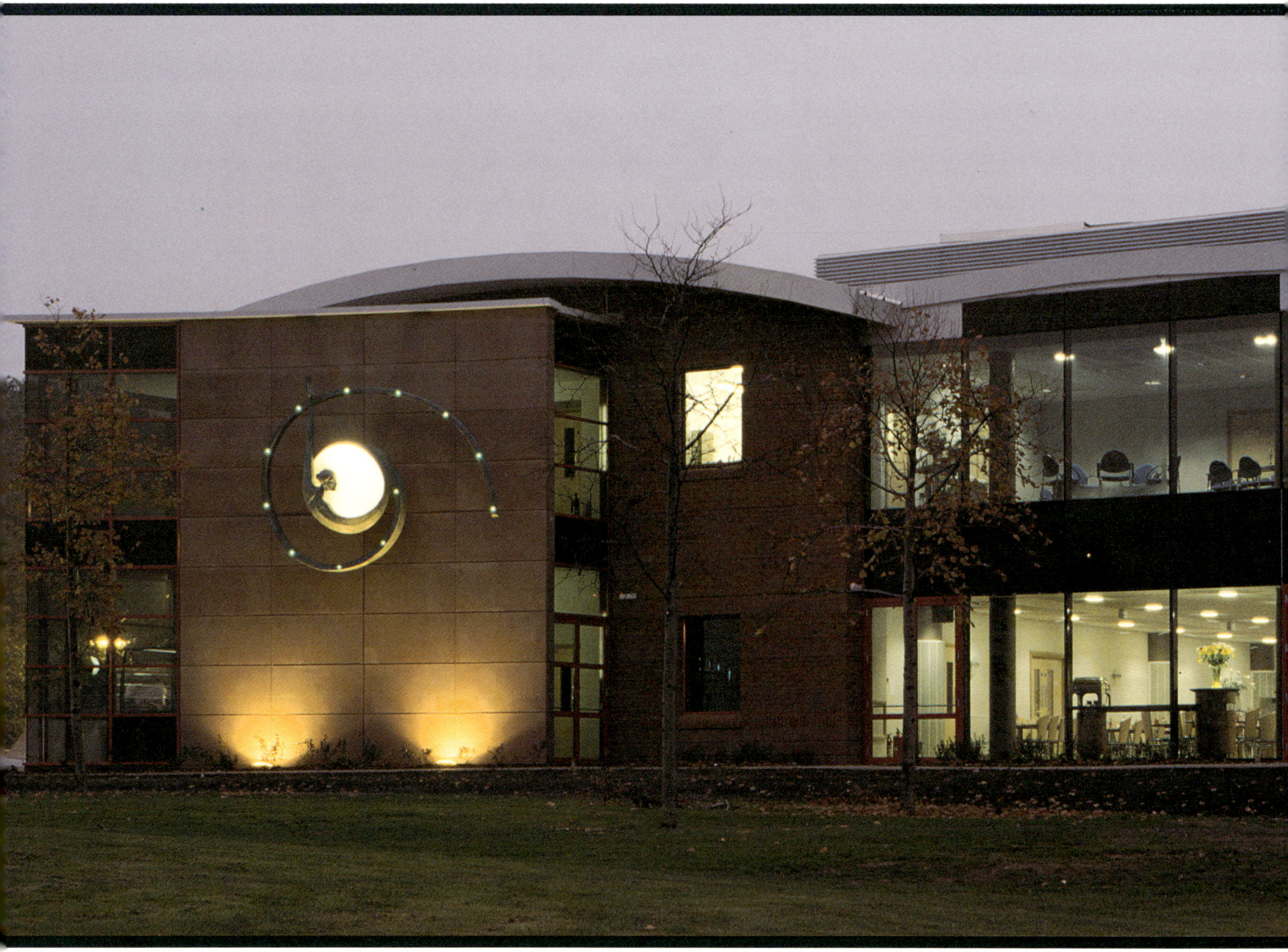

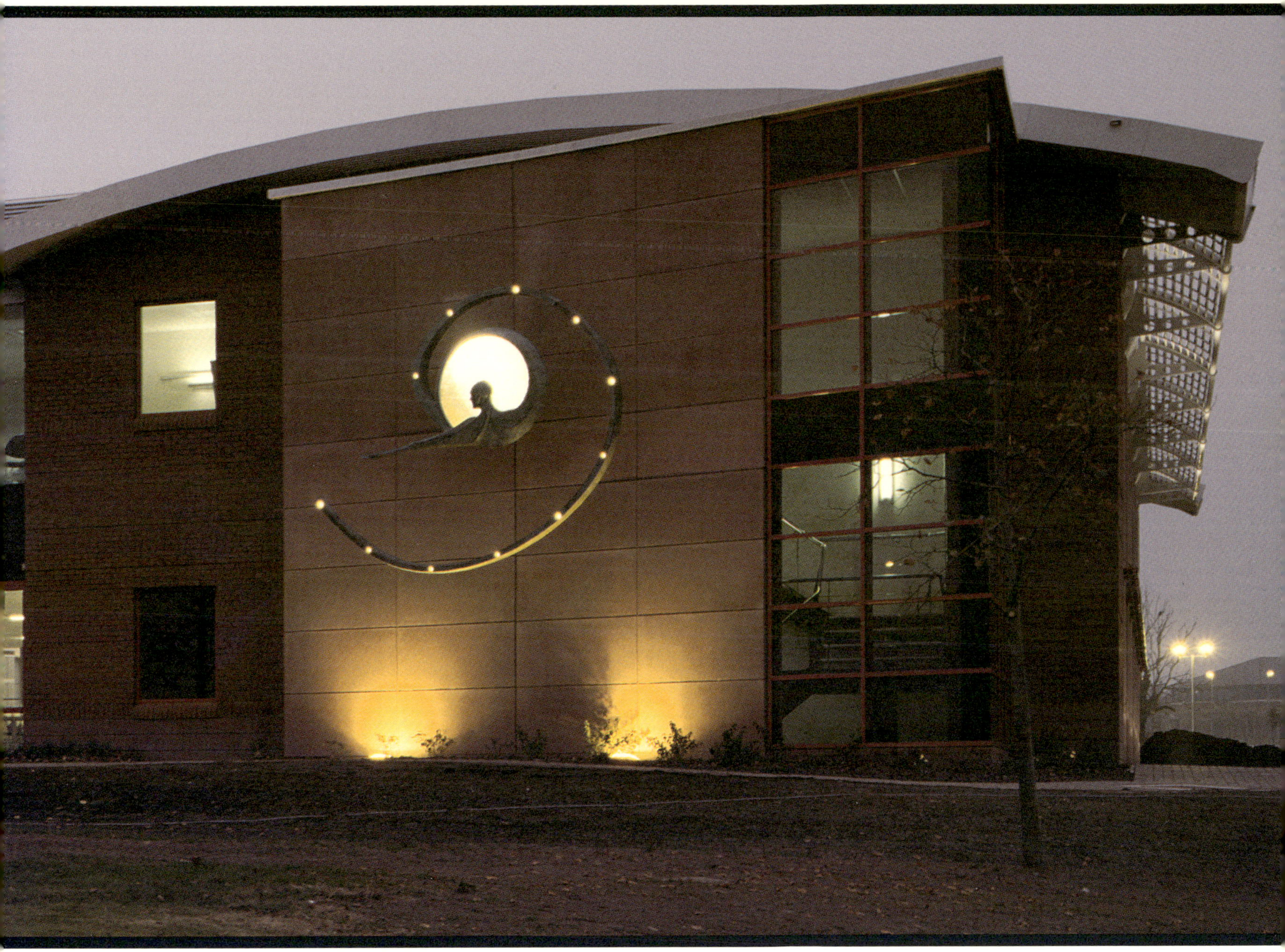

Foundation Building, CAPITAL BANK plc, Chester. Unveiled December 1997

CAPITAL BANK
A BANK OF SCOTLAND GROUP COMPANY

The production of this book was made possible by the kind assistance of CAPITAL BANK plc